THE

One-Dish Chicken

COOKBOOK

THE

One-Dish Chicken

COOKBOOK

Featuring

120

SOUPS, STEWS, CASSEROLES,
ROASTS, AND MORE
FROM AROUND THE WORLD

BROADWAY
BOOKS
NEW YORK

Mary Ellen Evans

BROADWAY

PRINTED IN THE UNITED STATES OF AMERICA

BROADWAY BOOKS and its logo, a letter B bisected on the
diagonal, are trademarks of Random House, Inc.

Visit our Web site at www.broadwaybooks.com

First edition published 2006

Book design by Elizabeth Rendfleisch

Library of Congress Cataloging-in-Publication Data

Evans, Mary Ellen, 1948–
The one-dish chicken cookbook : featuring 120 soups, stews,
casseroles, roasts, and more from around the world /
Mary Ellen Evans.—1st ed.
p.   cm.
Includes bibliographical references and index.
1. Cookery (Chicken)   2. Casserole cookery.
3. One-dish meals.   I. Title.
TX750.5.C45E956 2006
641.6'65—dc22   2005046972

ISBN 0-7679-1824-X

1   3   5   7   9   10   8   6   4   2

I dedicate this book
to my mother, Margaret,
who was a wonderful cook,
and to my father, Walter,
who loved good food.
They would have been so proud.

Contents

ACKNOWLEDGMENTS

My editor, Jennifer Josephy, and my agent, Stacey Glick, deserve many thanks.

My husband, Glen, and my children, Melanie and Eric, get many kudos for their patience and understanding while I put this book together and for being willing tasters. In addition, I appreciate all the support from friends, neighbors, and cooking students who were so generous with their encouragement over the year it took me to write this book.

Tucked in one of my kitchen cupboards is a stout, squat, earthenware stewpot. Its deep orange tint burnished from years of use dates its origins to the 1970s. Indeed, as a new bride, I purchased this pot as one of my first kitchen treasures. On a limited budget and still a student, I bought nothing lightly and conducted a substantial inner debate with myself whether I should spend my limited funds on what seemed a somewhat extravagant indulgence. I could have saved my time; the fact that I stood there conducting a cash-flow analysis all the while clutching the pot firmly in my grasp foretold the final decision. Eventually, the seemingly limitless possibilities for producing delectably inexpensive meals in one container proved too much of a temptation to resist.

My simple pot's seductive promise is one I'd like to share with you. It's a promise that's easily kept as I've found by experience over the years. Time and time again, I've stewed a cut-up chicken with wine, vegetables, and broth or with other equally agreeable combinations of ingredients and been rewarded with an entire main course for family or friends. Requiring little tending, this pot and other one-pot casseroles and cooking vessels continue to be a godsend in an ever more harried world. The succulently enticing smells of dinner permeate the house each time I take my pot from its storage space next to several others and fill it with market finds.

One of the most easily found treasures is a nice plump chicken, cut in pieces when destined for my well-used earthenware pot or other casseroles, left whole when added to my gleaming copper roaster, or sometimes bought in specific parts, such as all thighs or all breasts. No matter its form, chicken is always a reliable base for delightful dining. Enhanced by assorted seasonings, vegetables, grains, pasta, or potatoes, my feast is complete. For inspiration, I choose from the world's assortment of poultry treatments, chicken being a universal favorite. Using the globe as a source for flavor combinations and unusual cooking vessels adds additional interest to chicken, instead of the often insipid treatment to which this accessible bird is at times subjected. Sharing these casually upscale creations is what *The One-Dish Chicken Cookbook* is all about.

France's Henry IV knew the significance of chicken in his kingdom. When bartering with God for a longer life, he vowed that each peasant would find *"une poule dans son pot"*—a chicken in his pot—every Sunday. Whether he ever kept that promise is unknown but the idea came up again, this time during Herbert Hoover's 1928 campaign when he promised "a chicken in every pot and a car in every garage."

Chicken clearly has been a sought-after food source for centuries. We continue to value chicken today as much for its versatility and health aspects as for its good taste, and we consume more chicken than any other meat. The simplicity of one-pot cooking proves itself just as invaluable to the present-day cook as it did centuries ago. Just as the burnished orange color of my earthenware pot has come full circle to appear in countless twenty-first-century cooking catalogs, Henry's pot of chicken is as up-to-date as it can be.

You'll find that *The One-Dish Chicken Cookbook* takes the one-pot poultry meal to a global level, adding interest and a new dynamic to what could be a humdrum main dish.

Enhancing the convenience this style of cooking offers, each of the 120 recipes gives do-ahead suggestions, along with tips on accompaniments for entertaining or family dining. This culinary tour showcases deliciously dynamic recipes from the Americas to Asia, with stops in Africa and Europe along the way. Featuring stews, soups, casseroles, and stir-fries along with fondues, pies, and slow-cooked main-dish offerings, this book uses multiple cooking containers, starting with the basic Dutch oven and roaster, but expanding to tagines, woks, paella pans, and clay cookers, among others.

As a food writer and cooking teacher, but most of all as a home cook, I'm excited to share my collection of global one-pot recipes with other home cooks. Some will be familiar, others new discoveries, but all have my personal perspective that make them unique. I hope you will enjoy them in your kitchen as much as I have in mine, filling your own treasured pot with many delightful meals. It's this style of cooking that establishes culinary traditions in families over the years, keeping the promise of superbly satisfying dishes that beg to be made and made again.

THE

One-Dish Chicken

COOKBOOK

1 The Chicken and the Pot

The wealth of chicken recipes throughout the world proves the worth of this tasty and practical bird. In many cultures, chickens are prized possessions, contributing first eggs to the family diet and, finally, giving their all in a stewpot, cazuela, or tagine to produce one, or more, succulent meals. These birds, allowed to roam, develop a depth of flavor caged birds sorely lack. Because they are older, they're often also "sturdier," a euphemism for firm to tough flesh that requires long, slow cooking.

Because, here at home, the poultry that we cook and consume is bred to come to market with all possible speed, I've adapted the following recipes to suit domestically produced birds.

The most common size of chicken available for purchase is the broiler/fryer. Weighing in at 2.8 to about 4.5 pounds, dressed and ready for sale, with a life span of six to eight weeks, these tender youngsters take much less time to cook than most of their global cousins. Some of these chickens have more taste than others, and the old adage that you get what you pay for is often true. Simply put, the best chickens on the market today are certified organic, raised according to documented procedures and by set standards, fed organic grains and soybeans, and slaughtered in a specified manner. The next best choices are free range or vegetarian fed, almost universally delivering a tastier bird. One other desirable category is chickens that are kosher. These birds are fed, killed, and processed according to strict guidelines. This processing includes a salting, producing a bird that is, essentially, brined at purchase.

From this point, things start to slide. The remaining choices are "natural," meaning only that the chicken has been processed without antibiotics but guaranteeing nothing else, and, finally, the basic, mass-produced supermarket bird, whose life has not been anything to which a chicken would aspire.

The recipes in this book are designed for the easily found broiler/fryer-sized chickens, whether whole or in designated parts. Thighs, which hold up to longer cooking than breasts without drying out, are often the cut of choice. Do trim them of any excess fat before using. Keep in mind that pieces of chicken can be interchanged. One breast is approximately the equivalent of two thighs or a thigh and a drumstick. Breast meat requires more care; cook it until it is just done, removing it from the heat when it is no longer pink without letting it linger in the pan. Thighs and drumsticks require less attention.

If you have access to or a need to cook an older bird, such as a roasting or stewing hen, remember that the flesh needs a long exposure to low heat, great for moist cooking but not ideal for stir-fries or quicker sautés.

Once the chicken is bought, it's time to choose the pot. Probably the two most useful cooking containers a cook can choose are a Dutch oven and a large skillet. Get a good-sized Dutch oven—around 5 quarts—thick enough to stand up to a flame when sautéing but not so heavy that, when filled, it cannot be lifted. As for skillets, choose one that's about 12 inches in diameter at the top, of some substance and heft. I use two large 12-inch skillets in my kitchen, one with and one without nonstick coating. The one without browns better; the one with needs less fat and is also a great stand-in for a wok. Both have oven-proof handles, making them doubly useful.

Another handy skillet is the nonstick, 10-inch variety, great for cooking eggs or for sautéing smaller quantities.

Some other useful pots and pans from here and abroad are as follows.

ROASTER My roaster is a gem—thick, heavy, and large enough to hold an average-sized turkey. Its sides aren't too deep, allowing the oven heat to brown the roasting bird. Pans like this don't come cheaply but, once purchased, should last a lifetime.

BAKING PAN An assortment of ovenproof, metal and glass baking pans, especially one that measures around 13 × 9 inches, are useful pieces of equipment in a well-stocked kitchen. Look for pans that are made of thicker metal to prevent warping and burning. Relatively inexpensive Pyrex pans can be bought almost anywhere, even in well-stocked grocery stores.

WOK Popular throughout Asia, woks are available in two varieties. The round-bottomed model comes with a ring to funnel heat and hold the pan stable over the heat source. The flat-bottomed type rests right on the burner. Both work well. The rounded, deep sides provide lots of hot metal for quick cooking; the depth accommodates steamer baskets and cooking larger items, especially when covered by the wok's characteristically domed lid.

BROILER PAN   All ranges come with one; most cooks never use it, which is a pity. Broiling is like having a grill in your kitchen, allowing for quick cooking using direct heat. The pan is in two parts—a rectangular bottom that has shallow edges and that catches fat and juices, and a top section that is grooved and has rows of open slots to let accumulated fat and juices run off from whatever is cooking. The slots prevent any fat from pooling and catching on fire from close exposure to the heat, so it's important not to cover this top section with aluminum foil. Think about adding quick-cooking vegetables along with your chicken (or other meat or fish) when broiling for a one-pan cleanup.

PAELLA PAN   A paella pan, of Spanish origin, is a shallow, wide, round metal pan used for preparing recipes of the same name. It traditionally has two handles for lifting and is meant to stand up to direct heat.

CAZUELA   A cazuela is simply a round earthenware casserole, shallower in Spain and deeper in Latin America. This is a great baking dish, best soaked for a few hours before using the first time.

CLAY BAKER   Clay bakers are oval, lidded baking containers that collect moisture on the lid, which then bastes the food that's cooking. Directions vary by manufacturer, but most need to be soaked in water before using and most go into a cold oven, which is then set to a fairly high temperature.

TAGINE   A tagine is also a lidded, earthenware cooking vessel, with a shallow, round base and a conical top, used to cook recipes of the same name. From North Africa, tagines were intended to cook foods slowly over a brazier; their conical lids also trap moisture and return the condensed steam to the ingredients below.

SLOW COOKER   A modern invention for a centuries-old idea, slow cookers are electric, ceramic, lidded cookers designed to heat food over extended periods of time, often while the cook is at work. They work best with tougher cuts of poultry and meat, sometimes overcooking chicken, but still a useful tool. Remember when adapting traditional recipes for the slow cooker that these pots need far less liquid than normal. Instead, they generate extra liquid from the food as it cooks.

PRESSURE COOKER Pressure cookers do exactly what their name implies—cook food under pressure. While heating, they develop a seal and cook the enclosed ingredients rapidly while maintaining moisture. Older pressure cookers inspired fear in many users; modern cookers are very safe.

FONDUE POT Trendy in the 1970s and popular once again, fondue pots come from Switzerland and are an enjoyable way for everyone to cook tableside. The pot itself is filled with hot oil or broth and ingredients are dipped in the pot to cook. Sometimes the pot is filled with a molten Swiss cheese mixture or chocolate for dipping. Some fondue pots rely on petroleum chafing-dish fuel; some are electric.

As you can see, the selection of pots is extensive. Made of metal, clay, and glass and meant for heating via flame, charcoal, or indirect oven baking, the choices are as broad as the recipes to put in them. One-pot cooking offers endless possibilities. So, choose your chicken, choose your pot, and explore the world.

2 Soups

othing fancy, nothing hard—this dish is simply good, satisfying soup, Chinese-style. The snow peas add color and crunch to the basic, egg-laced broth, and the diced chicken adds a bit of substance to a quickly made lunch, simple supper, or even a nontraditional breakfast.

Chicken Egg Drop Soup

MAKES 4 SERVINGS

✳

4 CUPS REDUCED-SODIUM CHICKEN BROTH

TWO 6-OUNCE BONELESS, SKINLESS CHICKEN BREAST HALVES

4 QUARTER-SIZED GINGER SLICES, LIGHTLY SMASHED WITH A KNIFE

2 TABLESPOONS CORNSTARCH

2 LARGE EGGS, BEATEN UNTIL BLENDED BUT NOT FOAMY

4 OUNCES SNOW PEAS, CUT ON THE DIAGONAL IN 1/8-INCH SLIVERS (ABOUT 1 1/2 CUPS)

2 GREEN ONIONS, WHITE AND TENDER GREEN PORTIONS, CUT ON THE DIAGONAL IN THIN SLICES

Bring the chicken broth, chicken, and ginger slices just to a boil in a large saucepan over medium heat. Reduce the heat to low and cook until the chicken is no longer pink in the thickest portion when cut with a knife, about 15 minutes.

Remove the pan from the heat. Remove the chicken and ginger from the broth; discard the ginger. Skim off any foam from the broth. Let the chicken cool slightly and cut in 1/2-inch dice; set aside.

Return the pan with the broth to the heat and bring to a boil. Dissolve the cornstarch in 2 tablespoons water in a small bowl; stir into the broth. Boil until slightly thickened and clear, about 1 minute. Reduce the heat to medium-low so the broth is at a simmer. Using a chopstick, stir the broth while slowly pouring in about one-third of the eggs to form scrambled threads; repeat twice with the remaining eggs. Add the diced chicken, snow peas, and green onions; return to the simmer and cook for 2 minutes.

MAKE AHEAD Cook the chicken in the broth ahead of time and finish the recipe just before serving.

SERVE WITH Because this unpretentious dish is best served when a light meal is all that's required, it really needs no accompaniments.

*T*raveling through China, we ate these broth-based and cornstarch-thickened soups time and time again. The vegetables varied, but one of my favorites was the version with corn. Perhaps my Midwestern heritage prejudiced me, but I loved the saltiness of the broth combined with the sweetness of the corn. I've changed things a bit to make this more of a main-course offering. Puréeing some of the soup adds body, and I've added a bit more smoked chicken than usual. Playing with the citrus accents of lemongrass and the zing of ginger, I've added a subtle, underlying layer to the finished flavor.

Chinese Chicken-Corn Soup

MAKES 4 SERVINGS

❈

3 GINGER SLICES, PLUS
1/2 TEASPOON MINCED GINGER

2 GREEN ONIONS

2 LEMONGRASS STALKS,
TRIMMED

4 CUPS REDUCED-SODIUM
CHICKEN BROTH

2 LARGE EGG WHITES

1 TABLESPOON CORNSTARCH

1 1/2 CUPS FRESH CORN
KERNELS (OR FROZEN AND
THAWED)

1/2 CUP DICED SMOKED
CHICKEN, TURKEY, OR HAM

Tap the ginger slices with the flat side of a knife blade to smash; place in a Dutch oven. Thinly slice 2 teaspoons of the tender green portion of the green onions and set aside. Add the remaining white and pale green portions to the Dutch oven. Tap the lemongrass stalks with the flat side of a knife blade to smash; add to the Dutch oven. Add the chicken broth; heat over medium-high heat until the mixture just comes to a boil. Reduce the heat to low; cook for 10 minutes, uncovered.

Meanwhile, whisk the egg whites with 2 tablespoons water in a medium bowl until frothy; set aside. Stir the cornstarch together with 2 tablespoons water in a small bowl; set aside.

When the broth has simmered for 10 minutes; remove the ginger slices, onion pieces, and lemongrass; discard. Stir in the corn kernels. Remove 1 cup of the corn-broth mixture; purée in a blender. Return the mixture to the Dutch oven. Heat over medium heat; stir in the minced ginger and the dissolved cornstarch mixture. Bring to a boil, stirring often. Boil to thicken the mixture slightly, about 1 minute. Remove from the heat and stir in the egg white mixture with only a few stirs. Stir in the smoked chicken and serve immediately, garnished with the reserved sliced green onions.

MAKE AHEAD Prepare the soup up to adding the diced smoked chicken. When ready to rewarm, do so gently over medium-low heat. When hot, stir in the smoked chicken, top with the sliced green onions, and serve.

SERVE WITH A green salad tossed with an orange-spiked vinaigrette plus sesame-topped crusty rolls.

A vgolemono is a classic Greek soup, known by its lemony taste and egg-enriched chicken broth. I've added chunks of chicken and asparagus to make a complete, one-soup-pot meal.

Avgolemono Chicken Soup

MAKES 4 SERVINGS

※

5 CUPS REDUCED-SODIUM
CHICKEN BROTH

1/3 CUP LONG-GRAIN RICE

1 POUND ASPARAGUS, TRIMMED
AND CUT IN 1 1/2-INCH PIECES

1/2 CUP CHOPPED FRESH
DILL WEED

1/4 TEASPOON FRESHLY
GROUND PEPPER

2 LARGE EGG YOLKS

3 TABLESPOONS LEMON JUICE

2 CUPS COOKED, DICED
CHICKEN

Bring the chicken broth just to a boil in a Dutch oven over medium-high heat. Stir in the rice; reduce the heat to low and simmer, partially covered, for 20 minutes. Add the asparagus, 1/4 cup of the dill, and the pepper during the last 5 to 8 minutes of cooking. (Thicker asparagus will take slightly longer to cook than thinner spears.) Remove from the heat.

Whisk the egg yolks and lemon juice together in a medium bowl. Pushing the asparagus aside with a slotted spoon, ladle out 1 1/2 cups of broth from the Dutch oven. (Don't worry about any rice that comes up with the broth.) Slowly whisk the hot broth into the egg mixture and then whisk the broth-egg mixture back into the rest of the soup in the Dutch oven. Return the soup to low heat; add the chicken and the remaining 1/4 cup dill; cook, stirring constantly, until piping hot but not boiling, 5 to 8 minutes.

MAKE AHEAD Prepare this recipe up to the point of whisking the broth into the egg mixture. Refrigerate, covered, until ready to reheat. Bring the soup back to a simmer, then proceed with the recipe as written.

SERVE WITH Sliced tomatoes sprinkled with feta and drizzled with olive oil plus crusty bread or pita.

Quaintly named from the cooking pot's contents—namely a rooster, or cock, and a generous amount of leeks—cock-a-leekie soup most likely dates back to early Scottish cooking. Older versions also include a piece of beef along with the chicken, in much the same manner as pot-au-feu, and add prunes toward the end of the cooking time, for a somewhat incongruous touch. I've updated the recipe, omitting the prunes and adding potatoes, whose affinity for leeks is well established in vichyssoise, the French leek-and-potato soup. This sturdily satisfying soup gains sparks of bright orange color from the carrots and pale green from the second addition of leeks.

Cock-A-Leekie Soup

MAKES 6 SERVINGS

❋

1 TABLESPOON CANOLA OIL

1 TABLESPOON SALTED BUTTER

4 MEDIUM LEEKS, WHITE AND PALE GREEN PORTIONS, TRIMMED, HALVED, THOROUGHLY RINSED, AND CUT IN 1/2-INCH DICE (ABOUT 4 CUPS)

6 BONE-IN, SKIN-ON CHICKEN THIGHS

3 CUPS REDUCED-SODIUM CHICKEN BROTH

2 THYME SPRIGS

2 PARSLEY SPRIGS

1 BAY LEAF

4 SMALL RED BOILING POTATOES (ABOUT 1/2 POUND), PEELED AND CUT IN 1/2-INCH DICE (ABOUT 1 1/2 CUPS)

2 MEDIUM CARROTS, PEELED AND CUT IN 1/2-INCH DICE (ABOUT 1 CUP)

1/4 TEASPOON SALT

1/8 TEASPOON FRESHLY GROUND PEPPER

Heat the canola oil and butter in a Dutch oven over medium heat; when sizzling, stir in all but 1 cup of the leeks. Sauté the leeks until beginning to soften, 3 to 4 minutes. Add the chicken, chicken broth, and 3 cups water. Bring just to a boil; reduce the heat to low and simmer for 10 minutes. Spoon off any surface foam; add the thyme, parsley, and bay leaf tied together with string (bouquet garni). Continue to simmer for an additional 50 minutes, partially covered.

Remove the chicken to a plate to cool slightly; remove and discard the bouquet garni. Add the potatoes, carrots, and salt to the soup; adjust the heat to maintain a simmer. Simmer for 30 minutes.

Meanwhile, remove the skin and bones from the chicken and cut in bite-sized pieces. Add to the simmering soup during the last 10 minutes of cooking time along with the remaining 1 cup leeks. Stir in the pepper just before serving.

MAKE AHEAD This recipe can be made fully ahead and gently reheated over medium-low heat until piping hot, about 20 minutes. It can be made a day or two in advance and stored, covered, in the refrigerator.

SERVE WITH A tossed salad with a simple coarse-ground mustard vinaigrette and some crusty multigrain rolls. Add a block of aged Cheddar or Wensleydale cheese, either to eat in comforting chunks with the soup or afterward, and serve a spot of English ale, if desired.

While other cultures make a poultry-based soup with noodles, I think of chicken noodle soup as being quintessentially American, right up there with pot roast and apple pie. Putting the canned version to shame, a bowl of this homemade broth full of vegetables, poached chicken, and homemade egg noodles brings on a smile of pleasure that starts with the first sip and stays to the last drop.

Chicken Noodle Soup

MAKES 6 SERVINGS

❉

1 LARGE LEEK, WHITE AND PALE GREEN PORTIONS, TRIMMED, HALVED, AND THOROUGHLY RINSED

2 POUNDS CHICKEN WINGS

1 BAY LEAF

2 TEASPOONS SALT

$1/2$ TEASPOON DRIED THYME

4 BONELESS, SKINLESS CHICKEN THIGHS

$2/3$ CUP ALL-PURPOSE FLOUR

1 LARGE EGG

2 MEDIUM CARROTS, PEELED AND CHOPPED (ABOUT 1 CUP)

2 LARGE CELERY STALKS, CHOPPED (ABOUT 1 CUP)

$1/4$ TEASPOON FRESHLY GROUND PEPPER

Place the pale green portion of the leek, cut in chunks, in a Dutch oven; chop the white portion and reserve. Add the chicken wings, bay leaf, salt, and $1/4$ teaspoon of the thyme to the pot. Add 8 cups water; bring just to a boil over medium-high heat. Reduce the heat to low and cook, partially covered, for 30 minutes. Add the chicken thighs and cook for an additional 30 minutes. Strain, reserving the broth. Set the thighs aside to cool. Discard the wings, cooked leek, and bay leaf. Skim off the fat from the broth; reserve 1 tablespoon.

Meanwhile, for the noodles, process the flour and the egg in the bowl of a food processor fitted with a metal blade for 10 seconds. Turn out onto a counter and gather into a ball. Knead briefly, about 10 turns, with a scant amount of flour if sticky. Let rest, covered, for 30 minutes.

Cut the cooled thighs in bite-sized pieces.

Heat the reserved 1 tablespoon chicken fat in the same Dutch oven over medium-low heat. Add the chopped white portion of the leek, the carrots, and celery. Sauté until softened, about 5 minutes. Add the reserved broth and bring it back to a simmer; cook for 10 minutes.

While the vegetables are cooking in the broth, roll out the noodle dough on a lightly floured surface until about $^1/16$ inch thick. Cut into strips about $1^1/2 \times {}^1/2$ inch. Dust the strips very lightly with flour to keep them from sticking together.

After the vegetables have cooked in the broth for 10 minutes, add the thigh pieces to the pot. When the liquid returns to a simmer, add the noodles. Cook for 5 minutes. Stir in the remaining $^1/4$ teaspoon thyme and the pepper; serve.

MAKE AHEAD The entire recipe can be made ahead and refrigerated, covered. Reheat the soup over medium-low heat until just simmering.

SERVE WITH Thick slices of oven-warmed bread and a green salad for a simple but satisfying supper.

This recipe, without a doubt, is Jewish comfort food in a bowl. The matzoh balls are simultaneously light and filling; the broth is delicious in and of itself and is almost identical to the formula I included in my book *Bistro Chicken*.

For a simplified version, use prepared chicken broth.

Matzoh Ball Soup

MAKES 8 SERVINGS

✳

CHICKEN BROTH

3 1/2 TO 4 POUNDS CHICKEN
PIECES, KOSHER IF DESIRED,
ANY LIVER REMOVED AND
RESERVED FOR ANOTHER USE

2 MEDIUM CARROTS, PEELED
AND QUARTERED

1 MEDIUM ONION, QUARTERED

1 LARGE CELERY STALK WITH
LEAFY TOP, QUARTERED

6 PARSLEY SPRIGS

1/4 TEASPOON DRIED
THYME

1 BAY LEAF

8 BLACK PEPPERCORNS

2 TEASPOONS SALT

For the broth, place the chicken in a large Dutch oven or stockpot and cover with 3 quarts cold water. Bring just to a boil over medium-high heat, 10 to 15 minutes. Reduce the heat to medium-low to maintain a simmer; simmer for 10 minutes. Skim to remove any surface foam; add the carrots, onion, celery, parsley, thyme, bay leaf, peppercorns, and salt. Reduce the heat to low; cook, partially covered, for 2 1/2 hours, adjusting the heat as necessary so that the surface is broken only by occasional bubbles. Strain and discard the chicken, vegetables, and seasonings. Remove the surface fat; reserve 3 tablespoons. Refrigerate the broth until ready to use. (If made the day before, wait to skim the solidified fat from the surface once chilled.) Makes about 8 cups broth.

For the matzoh balls, whisk the eggs in a medium bowl until well blended; whisk in the reserved chicken fat and sparkling water. Stir in the matzoh meal, the 2 tablespoons chives, 1 tablespoon of the parsley, the salt, and pepper. Refrigerate the mixture for 3 hours.

Bring 3 quarts salted water to a boil over high heat in a large Dutch oven. With wet hands, shape the matzoh mixture into 16 small balls. Drop the balls into the boiling water and reduce the heat to low. Simmer, covered, for 20 minutes. Remove with a slotted spoon. Pour out the water.

Reheat the broth in the same Dutch oven. Place 2 matzoh balls in each of 8 bowls; ladle the broth over the balls. Combine the remaining 1 teaspoon chives and 1 tablespoon parsley in a small bowl; sprinkle $^1/_2$ teaspoon over each bowl of soup and serve.

MAKE AHEAD Prepare the broth and the matzoh balls. Refrigerate each separately, covered, then add the matzoh balls to the soup to reheat—5 to 8 minutes once the broth is simmering.

SERVE WITH Matzoh ball soup stands alone, a bowl of sustenance and warmth that needs nothing else.

MATZOH BALLS

3 LARGE EGGS

3 TABLESPOONS CHICKEN FAT, SKIMMED FROM THE BROTH

3 TABLESPOONS SPARKLING WATER

$^3/_4$ CUP MATZOH MEAL

2 TABLESPOONS PLUS 1 TEASPOON CHOPPED FRESH CHIVES

2 TABLESPOONS CHOPPED FRESH PARSLEY

$1^1/_4$ TEASPOONS SALT

$^1/_8$ TEASPOON FRESHLY GROUND PEPPER

*T*hin noodle wrappers fold around a delicate shrimp filling to make wontons, the Chinese equivalent of ravioli. When simmered along with chicken and shiitake mushrooms, the result is a lovely light meal in a bowl.

Chicken Wonton Soup

✳

1/2 POUND RAW PEELED SHRIMP

1 TABLESPOON MINCED GREEN ONION, PLUS 2 TABLESPOONS THINLY SLICED GREEN ONION

1 TABLESPOON EGG WHITE (ABOUT HALF OF 1 LARGE EGG WHITE, WHISKED)

2 TEASPOONS PLUS 1 TABLESPOON SOY SAUCE

2 TEASPOONS PLUS 1 TABLESPOON SHERRY

2 TEASPOONS CORNSTARCH

1 TEASPOON FINELY MINCED GINGER

1/2 TEASPOON SALT

16 WONTON WRAPPERS

6 CUPS REDUCED-SODIUM CHICKEN BROTH

2 OUNCES FRESH SHIITAKE MUSHROOMS, STEMS REMOVED AND CAPS THINLY SLICED (ABOUT 1 CUP)

1/8 TEASPOOOON GROUND WHITE PEPPER

TWO 6-OUNCE BONELESS, SKINLESS CHICKEN BREAST HALVES, THINLY SLICED

4 OUNCES SUGAR SNAP PEAS (ABOUT 1 CUP)

1 TEASPOON TOASTED SESAME OIL

Finely chop the shrimp; stir together with the minced green onion, egg white, 2 teaspoons soy sauce, 2 teaspoons sherry, 1 teaspoon of the cornstarch, the ginger, and salt in a small bowl. Fill a small, shallow bowl half full of water. Lay one wonton wrapper flat on the counter; spoon one-sixteenth, about 2 teaspoons, of the shrimp mixture into the center of each wonton wrapper. Dip a finger into the water and run it around two adjacent edges of the wrapper to moisten; fold the other two sides over to form a triangle and press to seal. Draw the two points of the base together; moisten slightly and press to seal. Repeat with the remaining wrappers.

Meanwhile, bring about 1 quart water to a boil in a large saucepan over medium heat. Add the filled wontons and bring back to a boil. Add 1/3 cup cold water and bring back to a boil again; boil for 1 minute and drain. Cover the drained wontons with cold water in a medium bowl to keep them from sticking together.

Bring the chicken broth and mushrooms to a boil over medium heat; reduce the heat to medium-low. Add the remaining 1 tablespoon soy sauce, remaining 1 tablespoon sherry, and the white pepper. Sprinkle the chicken with the remaining 1 teaspoon cornstarch and rub to coat. Add the chicken to the broth and bring back to simmer. Drain the wontons and add to the pan along with the sugar snap peas. Bring back to a simmer again and simmer for 1 minute. Stir in the sesame oil. Ladle into bowls and garnish with the sliced green onion.

MAKE AHEAD Prepare and poach the wontons, then hold them in water in the refrigerator until ready to proceed. Complete the recipe as directed when ready.

I love this south of the border version of chicken soup. Our northern version uses noodles; the Mexicans add leftover corn tortillas instead.

Tortilla Soup

MAKES 6 SERVINGS

✳

1/3 cup canola oil

4 stale corn tortillas, cut in half, then in 1/2-inch strips

2 dried ancho chiles, stemmed and broken in 1-inch pieces

1 medium onion, chopped (about 3/4 cup)

3 medium garlic cloves, minced (about 2 teaspoons)

3/4 teaspoon ground cumin

1/2 cup raw rice

5 cups reduced-sodium chicken broth

one 14 1/2-ounce can diced tomatoes in juice

one 4 1/2-ounce can diced green chiles

1 1/2 cups cooked, diced chicken

4 ounces monterey jack, shredded (about 1 cup)

2 tablespoons cilantro leaves

6 lime wedges

Heat the canola oil in the bottom of a Dutch oven over medium-high heat. Fry the tortilla strips in batches until crisp, about 2 minutes, stirring occasionally. Drain on paper towels; reserve. Add the ancho chile pieces to the oil; fry for about 30 seconds, stirring. Remove and set aside.

Pour out all but 2 tablespoons of the oil; add the onion. Reduce the heat to medium-low; sauté until softened, 6 to 8 minutes. Add the garlic and cumin; sauté until fragrant, 30 seconds to 1 minute. Add the rice; sauté, stirring often, until milky, 4 to 5 minutes. Add the chicken broth, the tomatoes with their juice, and the chiles; reduce the heat to low and simmer for 20 minutes. Stir in the chicken.

To serve, divide the cheese and tortilla strips among 6 bowls. Ladle the soup into bowls; garnish with the cilantro. Serve with the lime wedges on the side.

MAKE AHEAD Have the tortillas strips fried ahead. Complete the recipe through cooking the rice with the broth, tomatoes, and diced chiles, but only simmer the mixture for 15 minutes. Refrigerate the soup, covered, until ready to serve. Reheat over low heat; add the chicken.

SERVE WITH Sliced avocados scattered over mixed greens and warm, fresh tortillas to make the meal complete.

*A*dding chicken instead of the more traditional beef makes this version of borscht a bit lighter but no less delicious.

Chicken Borscht

MAKES 8 SERVINGS

✳

4 BONE-IN, SKIN-ON
CHICKEN THIGHS

ONE 14-OUNCE CAN
REDUCED-SODIUM
CHICKEN BROTH

ONE 14^1/$_2$-OUNCE CAN DICED
TOMATOES IN JUICE

1 POUND BEETS, PEELED AND
CUT IN ^{3}/$_4$-INCH DICE

4 SMALL POTATOES
(ABOUT ^{1}/$_2$ POUND), PEELED
AND CUT IN ^{3}/$_4$-INCH PIECES
(ABOUT 1^1/$_2$ CUPS)

2 MEDIUM CARROTS, PEELED
AND CUT IN ^{3}/$_4$-INCH PIECES
(ABOUT 1 CUP)

1 CUP SHREDDED
GREEN CABBAGE,
CUT IN 1 × ^{1}/$_2$-INCH SHREDS

2 MEDIUM CELERY STALKS,
CUT IN ^{1}/$_2$-INCH DICE
(ABOUT ^{2}/$_3$ CUP)

1 SMALL ONION, CHOPPED
(ABOUT ^{1}/$_2$ CUP)

2 TABLESPOONS
RED WINE VINEGAR

3/4 TEASPOON SALT

^{1}/$_4$ TEASPOON FRESHLY
GROUND PEPPER

PINCH GROUND CLOVES

2 TABLESPOONS CHOPPED
FRESH DILL WEED

Place the chicken in a Dutch oven; add the broth and 3 cups water. Bring just to a boil over medium heat. Reduce the heat to low; simmer, uncovered, for 1 hour. Remove the thighs and set aside.

Add the tomatoes and their juice to the Dutch oven along with the beets, potatoes, carrots, cabbage, celery, onions, red wine vinegar, salt, pepper, and cloves. Bring just to a boil; reduce the heat to low and cook, uncovered, until the vegetables are tender when pierced with the tip of a knife, 35 to 40 minutes.

Meanwhile, remove the skin and bones from the cooked chicken and discard. Cut the meat in bite-sized pieces. When the vegetables are tender, stir in the chicken and cook briefly to reheat the chicken, 2 to 3 minutes. Ladle into bowls and serve, garnished with the dill.

MAKE AHEAD Complete the recipe through cooking the vegetables until tender and cutting the chicken in pieces. Refrigerate the soup and the chicken separately, covered. When ready to serve, reheat the soup and then add the chicken as directed.

SERVE WITH A Russian rye bread for an excellent companion to the borscht.

When I travel, I often pack wild rice as gifts for my hosts abroad. It's indigenous to Minnesota and seems a unique introduction to North American cuisine. One of the better uses for this not-really rice (it's actually a grass) is in a creamy, chicken-laced soup. I've used crème fraîche because its sour yet slightly nutty taste is a pleasant echo of the wild-seed flavor found in these dark rice-shaped kernels.

Chicken and Wild Rice Soup

MAKES 4 SERVINGS

❋

TWO 6-OUNCE BONELESS, SKINLESS CHICKEN BREAST HALVES

3/4 CUP WILD RICE

3/4 TEASPOON SALT

3 TABLESPOONS SALTED BUTTER

1/3 CUP CHOPPED SHALLOTS

1/3 CUP ALL-PURPOSE FLOUR

TWO 14-OUNCE CANS REDUCED-SODIUM CHICKEN BROTH

1/2 CUP CRÈME FRAÎCHE

1 TABLESPOON PLUS 2 TEASPOONS CHOPPED FRESH TARRAGON

Place the chicken in a large saucepan or Dutch oven. Add 2 1/2 cups water and bring just to a boil over medium heat. Reduce the heat to low and simmer until the chicken is no longer pink when cut with a knife, about 15 minutes. Remove the chicken and let cool.

Add the wild rice and salt to the poaching liquid in the pan; bring just to a boil over medium heat. Reduce the heat to low and cook, covered, until the grains of rice have begun to open and the rice is chewy-tender, 1 to 1 1/4 hours.

Meanwhile, cut the cooled chicken in 1/2-inch cubes and place in a medium bowl.

When the rice is cooked, remove to the bowl with the chicken. Add the butter to the pan and melt over medium-low heat. Add the shallots and sauté until softened, about 5 minutes. Stir in the flour to form a paste; cook for 1 minute. Slowly whisk in the chicken broth; increase the heat to medium-high and bring to a boil. Boil until thickened, about 2 minutes. Reduce the heat to low; whisk in 1/4 cup of the crème fraîche until smooth. Add the 1 tablespoon tarragon; stir in the chicken and wild rice. Cook until heated through, 2 to 3 minutes. Ladle into bowls and top each bowl with 1 tablespoon of the remaining crème fraîche and $^1/_2$ teaspoon of the remaining tarragon.

MAKE AHEAD The soup can be made ahead and gently reheated. Don't heat it too long or the chicken will overcook. Once hot, ladle into bowls and top with the crème fraîche and tarragon as indicated.

SERVE WITH A simple tossed salad, sprinkled with toasted slivered almonds and garnished with a few spears of asparagus, if available, plus corn muffins.

*T*his is an elegant version of an American down-home favorite, all dressed up with breast meat, heavy cream, and dill. When corn season starts in Minnesota, stands selling ears of corn appear in the most unlikely urban settings—next to movie rental stores, florists, and anywhere there's a spare bit of pavement. The golden sweet kernels, on or off the cob, beg to be devoured; here, barely cooked, they are put to perfect use. In the winter, frozen corn makes a workmanlike substitute, reminding us of the warmth of summer.

I also prefer using dried dill weed when the weather turns cold. While fresh dill is far superior in the summer, the hothouse variety in grocery stores in midwinter is generally insipid, and a quality dried product turns out to be a better choice.

Chicken-Corn Chowder

MAKES 6 SERVINGS

❋

1½ TABLESPOONS CANOLA OIL

1 BACON SLICE, CUT IN ¼-INCH STRIPS

1 MEDIUM ONION, CHOPPED (ABOUT ¾ CUP)

TWO 14-OUNCE CANS REDUCED-SODIUM CHICKEN BROTH

2 MEDIUM RED BOILING POTATOES (ABOUT ½ POUND), PEELED AND CUT IN ½-INCH DICE

ONE 8-OUNCE BONELESS, SKINLESS CHICKEN BREAST HALF

4 CUPS FRESH CORN KERNELS (OR FROZEN AND THAWED)

½ CUP HEAVY CREAM

2 TABLESPOONS CHOPPED FRESH DILL WEED (OR 2 TEASPOONS DRIED DILL WEED)

Heat the oil in a Dutch oven over medium heat. Add the bacon; sauté until browned, 4 to 5 minutes. Remove with a slotted spoon; set aside.

Add the onion; sauté until softened, 4 to 5 minutes. Add the chicken broth, potatoes, and chicken; bring to a simmer. Reduce the heat to medium-low; simmer until the chicken is no longer pink in the center when cut with a knife, about 15 minutes.

Remove the chicken; set it aside to cool slightly. Remove the Dutch oven from the heat; stir in the corn.

Purée 2½ cups of the soup in a blender along with the cream; return to the Dutch oven. Stir in the dill. Bring to a simmer over medium heat.

Cut the chicken in ½-inch cubes; add to the Dutch oven along with the bacon pieces. Simmer to heat the chicken, 1 to 2 minutes. Serve.

MAKE AHEAD Make the recipe through puréeing the soup but don't add the cream. Refrigerate the soup and chicken separately. When ready to serve, add the cream and dill; bring to a simmer and add the chicken as directed.

SERVE WITH A tossed salad sprinkled with diced beets plus some crusty dinner rolls.

Chicken, two types of potatoes, cream, and capers come together in this Colombian soup, forming a unique combination of ingredients.

Typically, Ajiaco Bogotano calls for chunks of corn still on the cob, but this version uses totally edible baby corn for easier eating.

MAKES 4 SERVINGS

✳

6 BONE-IN, SKIN-ON
CHICKEN THIGHS

2 TEASPOONS SALT

$1/4$ TEASPOOOON GROUND CUMIN

$1/4$ TEASPOON DRIED
THYME

12 BLACK PEPPERCORNS

1 BAY LEAF

1 TABLESPOON CANOLA OIL

1 LARGE ONION, CHOPPED
(ABOUT $1^1/2$ CUPS)

2 MEDIUM-LARGE
RUSSET POTATOES (ABOUT
$1^1/4$ POUNDS), PEELED AND CUT
IN CHUNKS

4 MEDIUM RED BOILING
POTATOES (ABOUT 1 POUND),
PEELED AND CUT IN CHUNKS

ONE 14-OUNCE CAN BABY CORN,
DRAINED, RINSED, AND THE
EARS CUT IN HALF

$3/4$ CUP HEAVY CREAM

4 TEASPOONS NONPAREIL
CAPERS (IN VINEGAR), RINSED

1 LARGE AVOCADO, CUT IN
$1/2$-INCH DICE OR IN SLICES

CILANTRO LEAVES

Ajiaco Bogotano

(Colombian Chicken Soup)

Place the chicken in a Dutch oven and cover with 6 cups water. Add the salt, cumin, thyme, peppercorns, and bay leaf; bring just to a boil over medium-high heat. Reduce the heat to low and cook, partially covered, until the chicken is fork-tender, about 40 minutes. Strain into a large bowl; reserve the broth. Set the chicken aside to cool. Discard the bay leaf and peppercorns.

Wipe the Dutch oven dry with a paper towel. Heat the canola oil in the Dutch oven over medium heat; add the onion. Sauté until tender, 4 to 5 minutes. Return the broth to the Dutch oven; add the potatoes. Bring to a boil; reduce the heat to medium-low and cook until the potatoes are tender, about 20 minutes.

Meanwhile, remove the skin from the cooled chicken and discard. Remove the meat from the bones and cut the meat in bite-sized pieces.

When the potatoes are tender, purée with an immersion blender or mash with a potato masher until the soup is thickened. Add the corn and return the chicken to the Dutch oven; cook until heated through, 3 to 4 minutes.

Spoon 3 tablespoons cream in the bottom of each of 4 bowls; spoon 1 teaspoon capers into each bowl. Ladle the soup into the bowls. Garnish with the avocado and cilantro.

MAKE AHEAD Purée the soup as directed, then refrigerate the soup, covered, and the chicken and corn pieces, also covered, separately. When ready, reheat gently, then add the chicken and corn pieces. Proceed as directed.

SERVE WITH A jicama and orange salad and warm tortillas.

*L*ike a pizza bianco, this chili is called "white" because of the absence of any tomato products. Taken from the American Southwest, the poblano and Anaheim chiles, hominy, and beans add amazing depth to this one-pot meal.

MAKES 8 TO 10 SERVINGS

✳

FOUR 6- TO 8-OUNCE BONELESS, SKINLESS CHICKEN BREAST HALVES

ONE 14-OUNCE CAN REDUCED-SODIUM CHICKEN BROTH

2 POBLANO CHILES

2 ANAHEIM OR NEW MEXICO CHILES

2 TABLESPOONS SALTED BUTTER

2 TABLESPOONS CANOLA OIL

1 LARGE ONION, CHOPPED (ABOUT 1 1/2 CUPS)

1/4 CUP ALL-PURPOSE FLOUR

2 CUPS MILK

ONE 15 1/2-OUNCE CAN HOMINY, DRAINED AND RINSED

ONE 15 1/2-OUNCE CAN PINTO BEANS, DRAINED AND RINSED

ONE 15-OUNCE CAN GARBANZO BEANS, DRAINED AND RINSED

1 TABLESPOON CHILI POWDER

1 TABLESPOON GROUND CUMIN

1 TEASPOON SALT

3 TABLESPOONS WHITE CORNMEAL

1/2 CUP SOUR CREAM, PLUS ADDITIONAL FOR GARNISH

GRATED MONTEREY JACK OR CHEDDAR

SALSA VERDE

CILANTRO LEAVES

White Chicken Chili

Place the chicken in a large saucepan; add 2 cups water and the chicken broth. Bring just to a boil over medium heat; reduce the heat to low and simmer until the chicken is no longer pink in the thickest portion when cut with a knife, about 15 minutes. Remove and let cool; reserve the broth.

Meanwhile, toast the chiles over an open gas flame until the skin is charred on all sides; place in a bowl and cover with plastic wrap to steam for 5 minutes. (Alternatively, cut the chiles in half lengthwise and place, cut side down, on a shallow baking sheet. Broil until the skin is charred.) Remove from the bowl; scrape away the charred skin. Cut in half and remove the seeds and membranes. Cut in small dice and reserve.

Heat the butter and canola oil in a Dutch oven over medium-low heat. When sizzling, add the onion and sauté until softened, 6 to 8 minutes. Stir in the flour; cook, stirring often, for 2 minutes. Add the reserved broth; whisk to combine. Add the milk, hominy, pinto beans, garbanzo beans, reserved chiles, chili powder, cumin, and salt. Bring to a simmer and continue to simmer for 10 minutes.

Meanwhile, cut the cooled chicken in chunks.

Increase the heat to medium; add the chicken. Stir in the cornmeal and return the chili to a simmer; cook until slightly thickened, 2 to 3 minutes. Remove from the heat and stir in the $^1/_2$ cup sour cream. Serve in bowls with additional sour cream, grated cheese, salsa verde, and cilantro served separately as garnish.

MAKE AHEAD Make the chili to the point of returning the cooked chicken and thickening it with the cornmeal. Refrigerate it and the cooked chicken separately, covered, until ready to reheat. Gently reheat on medium-low heat, then increase the heat to medium. Add the chicken; stir in the cornmeal and proceed as directed.

SERVE WITH Warm tortillas plus an avocado-and-tomato-topped green salad.

Mulligatawny is the English version of *molagha tanni*, or pepper water, made into something quite different when brought back to the British Isles, more substantial than the original tart Indian broth laced with a bit of dal. I've added a few authentic notes to the British version, using tamarind paste and yellow split peas for dal.

MAKES 8 SERVINGS

✳

2 TABLESPOONS CANOLA OIL

1 LARGE ONION, CHOPPED
(ABOUT 1$\frac{1}{2}$ CUPS)

2 TABLESPOONS
MILD CURRY POWDER

1 TABLESPOON
CHOPPED GINGER

1 LARGE GARLIC CLOVE,
CHOPPED
(ABOUT 1$\frac{1}{2}$ TEASPOONS)

$\frac{1}{8}$ TEASPOON CAYENNE

6 BONE-IN, SKINLESS
CHICKEN THIGHS

$\frac{1}{3}$ CUP YELLOW SPLIT PEAS

1 TEASPOON TAMARIND PASTE

$\frac{1}{2}$ CUP BASMATI RICE

1 TEASPOON SALT

ONE 5$\frac{1}{2}$-OUNCE CAN
COCONUT MILK (OR $\frac{3}{4}$ CUP)

$\frac{1}{2}$ CUP PLAIN YOGURT

Mulligatawny Soup

Heat the canola oil in a Dutch oven over medium heat. Add the onion; sauté until softened, 4 to 5 minutes. Add the curry powder, ginger, garlic, and cayenne; sauté for 1 minute. Add the chicken and 6 cups water. Bring just to a boil; reduce the heat to low and add the yellow split peas. Cook, partially covered, for 40 minutes. Remove the chicken and let cool for about 10 minutes.

While the chicken is cooling, stir the tamarind paste into the broth to dissolve. Stir in the rice and salt. Cook, partially covered, for 15 minutes.

Remove the skin and bones from the chicken; cut the meat in chunks. Return the chunks of chicken to the pot along with the coconut milk and stir to blend. Ladle into bowls and serve each bowl topped with 1 tablespoon yogurt.

MAKE AHEAD Complete the recipe and refrigerate the soup, covered, until ready to serve. Reheat over low heat to a simmer; ladle into bowls and top with the yogurt.

SERVE WITH A tossed salad dressed with a lemon-based vinaigrette and toasted pita wedges.

3 Stews

*C*ombining the traditional *poule-au-pot* method of poaching a whole chicken in broth along with winter vegetables seems like just the thing to do. On a cold, crisp day, a steaming bowl of this glorious soup/stew makes a most satisfying meal.

Chicken in a Pot with Winter Vegetables

MAKES 6 SERVINGS

✳

ONE 5- TO 6-POUND CHICKEN

6 CUPS REDUCED-SODIUM CHICKEN BROTH

1 MEDIUM ONION, HALVED

4 CLOVES

10 BLACK PEPPERCORNS

4 FRESH SAGE LEAVES

3 PARSLEY SPRIGS

3 THYME SPRIGS

1 BAY LEAF

3/4 TEASPOON SALT

3 MEDIUM PARSNIPS, PEELED AND CUT IN 1^1/$_2$-INCH CHUNKS

2 MEDIUM CARROTS, PEELED, HALVED LENGTHWISE, AND CUT IN 1^1/$_2$-INCH CHUNKS

2 SMALL LEEKS, WHITE AND PALE GREEN PORTIONS, TRIMMED, HALVED, THOROUGHLY RINSED, AND CUT IN 1^1/$_2$-INCH PIECES

2 MEDIUM TURNIPS, PEELED AND CUT IN 1^1/$_2$-INCH CHUNKS

^{1}/$_2$ MEDIUM BUTTERNUT SQUASH, PEELED AND CUT IN 2-INCH CHUNKS

^{1}/$_2$ MEDIUM CELERY ROOT, PEELED AND CUT IN 1^1/$_2$-INCH CHUNKS

Truss the chicken; place in a small, deep stockpot or other flameproof pot large enough to hold all the ingredients but not excessively wide. Add the chicken broth and enough cold water to cover, an additional 6 to 8 cups. Bring almost to a boil over medium-high heat (large bubbles breaking the surface around the edges), 15 to 20 minutes, and reduce the heat to medium-low.

Gently simmer for 10 minutes, skimming off any surface foam. Add the onion halves stuck with the cloves, the peppercorns, sage, parsley, thyme, bay leaf, and salt. Reduce the heat to low; partially cover and barely simmer for 1 hour (1^1/$_2$ hours if using an older chicken).

Remove the chicken, using the trussing strings; let it drain over the pot and place it on a plate. Strain the broth through several layers of cheesecloth into a large bowl; discard the onion and poaching seasonings.

Return the chicken to the pot; add the parsnips, carrots, leeks, turnips, squash, and celery root. Pour in the strained broth. Heat over medium-high heat until just simmering. Reduce the heat to low and barely simmer, with the cover slightly ajar, until the vegetables are tender, 30 to 40 minutes. Remove the chicken and slice in large pieces. Return the chicken to the pot.

Alternatively, arrange the sliced pieces on a warm platter. Surround with the vegetables, removed from the broth with a slotted spoon. Pour the broth into a soup tureen, if desired. Serve the sliced chicken and vegetables in large, shallow bowls, such as soup bowls or pasta dishes, topped with broth.

MAKE AHEAD Prepare the entire recipe ahead, slice the chicken, and return it to the pot. Just before serving, warm the mixture gently over medium-low heat until piping hot, 20 to 30 minutes. Or, if desired, leave the chicken whole. Reheat the chicken, vegetables, and broth; remove and slice the chicken and serve with the vegetables separately on a platter as indicated.

SERVE WITH Crusty French bread. If serving for company, offer sliced hard sausage, pâté, and cornichon as an appetizer, a simple green salad as a first course, and a free-form apple tart for dessert.

My mother, a very good cook, used to make chicken topped with dumplings, and as a child I relished every bite of the fluffy, chicken broth–laced pillows of heaven. To this day, when I need to wrap myself in the cocoon of memory, nothing works quite as well.

Chicken and Dumplings

MAKES 4 SERVINGS

✳

1 TABLESPOON CANOLA OIL

2 MEDIUM CARROTS, PEELED AND CHOPPED (ABOUT 1 CUP)

1 MEDIUM ONION, CHOPPED (ABOUT 3/4 CUP)

1 MEDIUM CELERY STALK, CHOPPED (ABOUT 1/3 CUP)

1/2 TEASPOON DRIED, RUBBED SAGE

1/2 TEASPOON DRIED THYME

1/4 TEASPOON DRIED ROSEMARY, CRUMBLED

6 BONELESS, SKINLESS CHICKEN THIGHS, CUT IN BITE-SIZED PIECES

3 CUPS REDUCED-SODIUM CHICKEN BROTH

1 LARGE EGG

1 TABLESPOON SALTED BUTTER, MELTED

1/4 CUP MILK

1 CUP PLUS 2 TABLESPOONS SELF-RISING FLOUR, PREFERABLY WHITE LILY

Heat the canola oil in a Dutch oven over medium heat; add the carrots, onion, and celery. Sauté until softened, 4 to 5 minutes. Stir in the sage, thyme, and rosemary. Add the chicken; pour in the chicken broth. Reduce the heat to low and cook, covered, for 20 minutes.

Meanwhile, whisk the egg and melted butter together in a small bowl. Whisk in the milk. Put the flour into a medium bowl and make a well in the center. Stir in the egg mixture until blended into a dough.

After the chicken has simmered for 20 minutes, dip a tablespoon into the hot broth and then into the dough. Drop the spoonful of dough into the Dutch oven; continue with the rest of the dough, about 8 spoonfuls in all. Cook, covered, until the dumplings are fluffy, 20 minutes. Serve in shallow bowls.

MAKE AHEAD Prepare the recipe up through the initial 20-minute simmering of the thighs and broth. Make sure the chicken is no longer pink in the center when cut with a knife before refrigerating, covered, until ready to serve. Bring the mixture back to a simmer while preparing the dumpling dough, then proceed with the recipe as written.

SERVE WITH A simple green salad with cherry tomatoes for color and crunch.

oth the Cajuns and the French rely on roux as a thickener. While the term sounds fancy, roux is simply flour and fat cooked together. What makes the Cajun roux different is that oil replaces the butter found in French recipes, and the mixture is often cooked until it darkens, adding a pleasantly nutty, toasted undertone to the finished recipe. Along with a roux, the soup/stew called gumbo uses okra (or sometimes filé powder) for additional thickening.

Chicken Gumbo

MAKES 4 SERVINGS

✳

3 TABLESPOONS CANOLA OIL

6 BONELESS, SKINLESS CHICKEN THIGHS, CUT IN BITE-SIZED PIECES

1¹/₂ TEASPOONS CAJUN SEASONING

2 TABLESPOONS ALL-PURPOSE FLOUR

1 LARGE ONION, CHOPPED (ABOUT 1¹/₂ CUPS)

2 LARGE CELERY STALKS, CHOPPED (ABOUT 1 CUP)

1 GREEN BELL PEPPER, CHOPPED (ABOUT 1¹/₂ CUPS)

2 LARGE GARLIC CLOVES, MINCED (ABOUT 1 TABLESPOON)

TWO 14-OUNCE CANS REDUCED-SODIUM CHICKEN BROTH

1¹/₂ CUPS SLICED OKRA

3 CUPS COOKED RICE

Heat the canola oil in a Dutch oven over medium-high heat. Add the chicken in batches, seasoned with the Cajun seasoning; sauté until lightly browned, turning occasionally, 2 to 3 minutes per side. Remove the chicken with a slotted spoon; pour off the oil and reserve.

Clean the pan and return the reserved oil. Whisk in the flour. Heat over medium heat until the flour mixture (roux) is a medium brown, 3 to 5 minutes. Add the onion, celery, and bell pepper; reduce the heat to medium-low and sauté until softened, 6 to 8 minutes. Add the garlic; sauté until fragrant, 30 seconds to 1 minute. Return the chicken to the pan; add the chicken broth and okra. Bring just to a boil; reduce the heat to low and cook, uncovered, for 45 minutes.

Divide the rice among 4 large soup bowls or pasta bowls. Ladle the gumbo over the rice and serve.

MAKE AHEAD The gumbo can be made completely ahead, then reheated and ladled over the rice.

SERVE WITH Corn muffins and sliced tomatoes or a simple salad.

I like making this recipe with chicken thighs. Their sturdier texture is similar to the older hens or even the squirrel originally used in this Southern recipe. Lima beans give an authentic touch, and the surprise ingredient, ketchup, adds body and a touch of sweetness.

Brunswick Stew

MAKES 4 SERVINGS

❋

4 BACON SLICES, CUT IN
1/4-INCH STRIPS

1 LARGE ONION, CHOPPED
(ABOUT 1 1/2 CUPS)

2 LARGE CELERY STALKS,
CHOPPED (ABOUT 1 CUP)

1 TABLESPOON CANOLA OIL

8 BONE-IN, SKIN-ON
CHICKEN THIGHS

1/4 TEASPOON SALT

1/8 TEASPOON FRESHLY
GROUND PEPPER

ONE 15-OUNCE CAN
TOMATO SAUCE

1 CUP REDUCED-SODIUM
CHICKEN BROTH

1/2 CUP KETCHUP

2 TEASPOONS
WORCESTERSHIRE SAUCE

1 TEASPOON DRY MUSTARD

PINCH CAYENNE

4 MEDIUM-SMALL BOILING
POTATOES (ABOUT 3/4 POUND),
PEELED AND CUT IN
BITE-SIZED CHUNKS

ONE 9-OUNCE PACKAGE FROZEN
BABY LIMA BEANS, THAWED

1 1/2 CUPS FRESH
CORN KERNELS (OR FROZEN
AND THAWED)

Sauté the bacon in a Dutch oven over medium-high heat until lightly browned, stirring often, 5 to 7 minutes. Add the onion and celery; sauté until softened, scraping up any browned bits with a wooden spoon to prevent scorching, 3 to 4 minutes. Remove to a bowl. Add the canola oil. Sauté the chicken in batches, seasoned with the salt and pepper, until browned, 3 to 4 minutes per side. Remove and drain off the fat. Return the onion mixture with the chicken to the pot. Add the tomato sauce, chicken broth, ketchup, Worcestershire sauce, mustard, and cayenne to the pot; stir, scraping up any browned bits from the bottom of the Dutch oven. Add the potatoes; reduce the heat to low and cook, partially covered, until the chicken and potatoes are tender, about 40 minutes. Add the lima beans and corn; cook, partially covered, for 10 minutes.

MAKE AHEAD Make the whole recipe a day or two ahead of time, if desired; refrigerate, covered, until ready to reheat.

SERVE WITH Corn bread. That's all this hearty stew needs with everything already accounted for in the pot.

According to *The New Food Lover's Companion*, by Sharon Tyler Herbst, the term "burgoo" goes back to the 1700s when it was the name for a sailor's porridge. Now this one-pot meal is a Southern specialty, especially in Kentucky. Its very nature requires making large amounts; take it to potlucks or wherever a group of hearty eaters come together.

Kentucky Burgoo

MAKES 10 TO 12 SERVINGS

✳

1 TABLESPOON CANOLA OIL

4 OUNCES SALT PORK,
CUT IN 1 × 1/4-INCH STRIPS

1 POUND CUBED
BEEF STEW MEAT

1 TEASPOON SALT

1/2 TEASPOON FRESHLY
GROUND PEPPER

8 TO 10 BONELESS, SKINLESS
CHICKEN THIGHS,
CUT IN 2-INCH PIECES

2 CUPS TRIMMED OKRA
CUT IN 1-INCH PIECES

4 MEDIUM-SMALL RED BOILING
POTATOES (3/4 POUND), PEELED
AND CUT IN 3/4-INCH PIECES

3 MEDIUM CARROTS,
CUT IN 3/4-INCH PIECES

ONE 14 1/2-OUNCE CAN DICED
TOMATOES IN JUICE

ONE 9-OUNCE PACKAGE FROZEN
LIMA BEANS, THAWED

1 GREEN BELL PEPPER,
CUT IN 1/2-INCH DICE

1 MEDIUM ONION, CHOPPED
(ABOUT 3/4 CUP)

2 MEDIUM CELERY STALKS,
CUT IN 1/2-INCH SLICES

1/8 TEASPOON CRUSHED DRIED
RED PEPPER FLAKES

1 CUP FRESH CORN KERNELS
(OR FROZEN AND THAWED)

Heat the canola oil in a Dutch oven over medium-high heat. Add the salt pork strips; sauté until beginning to brown, 3 to 4 minutes. Add the cubes of beef; sauté until lightly browned on all sides, 6 to 8 minutes. Add 2 quarts water, the salt, and pepper. Bring just to a boil; reduce the heat to low and cook, partially covered, for 1 hour. Add the chicken and cook, partially covered, for 45 minutes. Add the okra, potatoes, carrots, tomatoes, lima beans, bell pepper, onion, celery, and pepper flakes. Increase the heat to medium and bring back to a simmer; reduce the heat to low and simmer, partially covered, until the okra and potatoes are tender, about 30 minutes. Stir in the corn kernels; cook for an additional 5 minutes. Ladle into bowls to serve.

MAKE AHEAD   This is easily made ahead from start to finish and then gently reheated.

SERVE WITH   Corn bread, soft dinner rolls, or fluffy biscuits. With all the vegetables, the stew doesn't even need a salad, although the fresh taste of crisp greens would make a nice contrast.

ingersnaps, traditionally added to pot roasts, provide extra body and zing to this stew already redolent with allspice, thyme, juniper, and gin. As in several other recipes, I've turned to crème fraîche. Its pleasantly nutty creaminess and ability to hold up to higher heat than sour cream make it a staple in my kitchen. To make your own crème fraîche, stir 1 cup of tepid heavy cream (not ultrapasteurized) and 2 tablespoons of buttermilk together in a bowl. Cover the mixture and let it rest at room temperature until the cream thickens, about 24 hours. Refrigerated, it thickens even more.

Gingersnap Stew

MAKES 4 SERVINGS

✳

1/2 TEASPOON SALT

1/2 TEASPOON DRIED THYME

1/4 TEASPOON FRESHLY GROUND PEPPER

1/4 TEASPOON GROUND ALLSPICE

ONE 3 1/2- TO 4-POUND CHICKEN, CUT IN PIECES

1 TABLESPOON CANOLA OIL

1 LARGE ONION, CHOPPED (ABOUT 1 1/2 CUPS)

1/2 CUP DICED HAM

1/4 CUP GIN

ONE 14-OUNCE CAN REDUCED-SODIUM CHICKEN BROTH

1 TABLESPOON WHITE WINE VINEGAR

8 JUNIPER BERRIES, CRUSHED

3/4 TEASPOON CARAWAY SEEDS

1/4 CUP CRÈME FRAÎCHE

8 GINGERSNAPS, CRUSHED INTO CRUMBS (ABOUT A SCANT 1/2 CUP)

Combine the salt, thyme, pepper, and allspice in a small bowl. Season the chicken with the spice mixture. Heat the canola oil in a Dutch oven over medium heat. Add the chicken in batches; sauté until well browned, about 5 minutes per side. Remove. Add the onion and ham; sauté until the onion is softened and beginning to brown, 4 to 5 minutes.

Return the chicken to the pan; pour the gin over the chicken and ignite. When the flames subside, add the chicken broth, vinegar, juniper berries, and caraway seeds; bring just to a boil. Reduce the heat to low and cook, partially covered, until the chicken is no longer pink in the thickest portion when cut with a knife, 45 to 50 minutes.

Remove the chicken; whisk the crème fraîche and crushed gingersnaps into the cooking liquid. Simmer until slightly thickened, 4 to 5 minutes. Return the chicken to the pan; turn to coat and serve.

Make the chicken up to the point of removing the chicken to add the crème fraîche and gingersnaps. Refrigerate, covered, until ready to serve, then reheat gently. Once hot, remove the chicken and add the crème fraîche and gingersnaps as directed.

SERVE WITH Potato pancakes topped with applesauce. Green beans make a good vegetable choice.

I came up with this version of coq au vin one day at my home in southern France. I used a local Côtes-du-Rhône wine from our friends the Tyrands, whose vineyard is right down the road from our village, Mollans. It combines both Provençal and Burgundian cooking styles in one tempting stew. Black olive paste adds an underlying of flavor and gives the sauce a deeper, darker, and more appealing color than the classic version.

Coq au Vin Chez Mary

MAKES 6 SERVINGS

❊

2 TABLESPOONS OLIVE OIL

4 OUNCES SALT PORK, CUT IN
1½ × ½-INCH STRIPS
(ABOUT 1 CUP)

1 POUND PEARL ONIONS,
PEELED (OR ONE 16-OUNCE BAG
OF FROZEN PEARL ONIONS,
THAWED)

3 BONE-IN, SKIN-ON CHICKEN
BREAST HALVES

3 BONE-IN, SKIN-ON
CHICKEN THIGHS

3 BONE-IN, SKIN-ON
CHICKEN DRUMSTICKS

¼ TEASPOON FRESHLY
GROUND PEPPER

8 OUNCES SMALL TO MEDIUM
MUSHROOMS, HALVED OR
QUARTERED

6 MEDIUM CARROTS, PEELED,
HALVED LENGTHWISE, AND CUT
IN 1-INCH PIECES

Heat 1 tablespoon of the olive oil in a Dutch oven over medium-high heat. Add the salt pork; sauté until crisp, 3 to 4 minutes. Remove with a slotted spoon. Add the onions; sauté until lightly browned, 5 to 6 minutes. Remove. Add the remaining 1 tablespoon olive oil. Add the chicken in batches, seasoned with the pepper; sauté until very well browned on both sides, 5 to 6 minutes per side. Remove. Add the mushrooms; sauté until beginning to soften, 3 to 4 minutes. Return the onions and the chicken to the Dutch oven; add the carrots. Pour in the red wine; stir in the olive paste, garlic, and herbes de Provence. Add the chicken broth. Bring just to a boil over medium heat; reduce the heat to low. Cook, partially covered, until the chicken is no longer pink in the thickest portion when cut with a knife, 50 to 60 minutes. Remove the chicken; cover with aluminum foil to keep warm.

Increase the heat to high and bring the liquid to a boil. Boil until reduced by about one-third, 8 to 10 minutes. Stir the cornstarch with 3 tablespoons cold water in a small bowl to dissolve; slowly whisk into the reduced liquid. Boil until slightly thickened, 1 to 2 minutes. Reduce the heat to medium-low; return the chicken to the Dutch oven and cook briefly to rewarm, 1 to 2 minutes.

MAKE AHEAD Make the entire stew ahead of time and simply reheat when ready.

SERVE WITH Lots of crusty French bread and greens tossed with an olive oil–based vinaigrette.

3 CUPS RED WINE

2 TABLESPOONS BLACK OLIVE PASTE (TAPENADE)

2 LARGE GARLIC CLOVES, CHOPPED (ABOUT 1 TABLESPOON)

1^1/$_2$ TEASPOONS HERBES DE PROVENCE

1^1/$_2$ CUPS REDUCED-SODIUM CHICKEN BROTH

3 TABLESPOONS CORNSTARCH

I'll never eat pot-au-feu without thinking of a small restaurant, not too far from Les Baux in France, called Bistrot du Paradou. One cold and rainy February day, my husband, Glen, and I stopped there for lunch. The chef serves only one dish each day. That day the choice was pot-au-feu. Preceded by a simple salad dressed with olive oil from nearby Maussane-les-Alpilles, this satisfying stew was just the thing. Warmed by the broth and the crackling fire in the adjoining room, we were fortified and ready to continue our damp journey.

Pot-au-feu can be made with or without chicken, but I like the contrast between the two meats in this recipe. If you have access to a stewing chicken, use about half of it and instead of taking the chicken out early and returning it late in the final cooking process, cook this tougher hen right along with the beef.

While easily made, this dish is best if started the day before you plan to serve it.

MAKES 6 SERVINGS

✳

6 BONE-IN, SKIN-ON CHICKEN THIGHS

2 POUNDS BONELESS CHUCK ROAST

2 LARGE ONIONS, HALVED LENGTHWISE

4 CLOVES

2 LARGE GARLIC CLOVES, PEELED AND LIGHTLY CRUSHED

1 TABLESPOON KOSHER OR COARSE SEA SALT, PLUS MORE AS AN ACCOMPANIMENT

6 PARSLEY STEMS

5 THYME SPRIGS (OR 1 TEASPOON DRIED THYME)

8 TO 10 BLACK PEPPERCORNS

3 MEDIUM CARROTS, PEELED AND CUT IN 2-INCH LENGTHS

Pot-au-Feu

Place the chicken and chuck roast in the bottom of a large Dutch oven. Add enough water to cover by 1 to 2 inches, 8 to 10 cups; heat just to a boil over medium heat. Reduce the heat to medium-low; simmer for 20 minutes, adjusting the heat as necessary to maintain a gentle simmer, and skimming off the surface foam.

Pierce each onion half with a clove; add to the pot. Add the garlic, salt, parsley, thyme, and peppercorns. Reduce the heat to low; simmer, partially covered, for 1 hour.

Remove the chicken; simmer the remaining ingredients for an additional 30 minutes. Remove the beef. Refrigerate the chicken and beef, covered, until ready to proceed. Strain the broth through several layers of cheesecloth; discard the onions, garlic, parsley, thyme, and peppercorns. Refrigerate the broth, covered, until chilled, several hours or overnight.

When ready to proceed, skim the congealed fat from the surface of the broth; return the broth to the pot along with the beef. Add the carrots, leeks, celery root, and turnip. Bring just to a boil over medium heat; reduce the heat to low and cook, partially covered, for 30 minutes. Add the potatoes; cook for 15 minutes. Add the chicken; cook for an additional 15 minutes.

Remove the chicken and beef from the pot; slice and arrange on a platter. Surround with the vegetables and spoon some of the broth over all. Serve the remaining broth in the pot or in a tureen. Serve the meats and vegetables together at the same time as the broth or serve the broth separately. Offer mustard, cornichons, and coarse salt as accompaniments.

MAKE AHEAD This recipe is inherently made in two parts. Completing the initial step the day before lets the broth chill properly and allows the cook to easily remove all the extra fat.

SERVE WITH Lots of crusty bread. Start with a salad dressed with extra virgin olive oil as my husband and I did in France, or follow the pot-au-feu with crisp greens tossed with a simple vinaigrette.

2 LEEKS, WHITE AND PALE GREEN PORTIONS, TRIMMED, HALVED, THOROUGHLY RINSED, AND CUT IN 2-INCH LENGTHS

1 SMALL CELERY ROOT, PEELED AND CUT IN 1½-INCH CHUNKS

1 LARGE TURNIP, PEELED AND CUT IN EIGHTHS

6 FINGERLING POTATOES, PEELED AND CUT IN HALF

COARSE MUSTARD

CORNICHONS

orcinis are substantial mushrooms with big, domed caps and fat stalks. Their taste is substantial, too, with big, rich, woodsy notes that add incredible depth to any recipe. Drying these mushrooms concentrates their essence even further, and since porcini mushrooms are seasonal, the dried version makes them accessible all year.

I've employed the useful trick of cooking ordinary button mushrooms with the soaking liquid from the dried porcinis. The liquid retains the strong flavor of the dried mushrooms and passes that flavor on to the blander white variety when they simmer together.

Chicken with Porcini Mushrooms

MAKES 6 SERVINGS

❇

1 CUP REDUCED-SODIUM CHICKEN BROTH

1 OUNCE DRIED PORCINI MUSHROOMS

2 TABLESPOONS OLIVE OIL

3 BONE-IN, SKIN-ON CHICKEN BREAST HALVES

3 BONE-IN, SKIN-ON CHICKEN THIGHS

3 BONE-IN, SKIN-ON CHICKEN DRUMSTICKS

1/2 TEASPOON SALT

1/4 TEASPOON FRESHLY GROUND PEPPER

1 LARGE ONION, CHOPPED (ABOUT 1 1/2 CUPS)

2 LARGE GARLIC CLOVES, CHOPPED (ABOUT 1 TABLESPOON)

Bring the chicken broth to a boil in a small saucepan over medium heat; remove from the heat. Stir in the dried porcini mushrooms; soak for 30 minutes. Remove with a slotted spoon; chop and reserve. Strain the soaking liquid through a coffee filter; reserve the strained liquid.

Heat the olive oil in a large Dutch oven over medium heat. Add the chicken in batches, seasoned with the salt and pepper; sauté until browned, 4 to 5 minutes per side. Remove.

Drain all but 2 tablespoons of the fat from the pot. Return to medium heat; add the onion and sauté until softened, 4 to 5 minutes. Add the garlic and sauté until fragrant, 30 seconds to 1 minute. Add the button mushrooms; sauté until they begin to soften, 3 to 4 minutes. Add the chopped porcini mushrooms and the soaking liquid; cook until the liquid has evaporated, 6 to 8 minutes. Stir in the rosemary; pour in the red wine. Chop the tomatoes in the can using kitchen shears; add to the pot. Return the chicken to the pot; turn gently to mix. Reduce the heat to low and simmer, partially covered, until the chicken is no longer pink in the thickest portion when cut with a knife, 45 to 50 minutes.

MAKE AHEAD Prepare the entire recipe ahead of time and reheat gently before serving.

SERVE WITH Polenta, bread, and a simple salad.

8 OUNCES WHITE BUTTON
MUSHROOMS, COARSELY
CHOPPED

2 TEASPOONS CHOPPED FRESH
ROSEMARY

$^1/_3$ CUP RED WINE

ONE 28-OUNCE CAN PLUM
TOMATOES

The term "puttanesca" refers to spicy ladies of easy virtue. One version of how this recipe got its name is that it was easy for these busy ladies to prepare; another suggests that the aroma alerted and lured customers to their location.

Chicken with Puttanesca Sauce

MAKES 6 SERVINGS

❋

2 TABLESPOONS OLIVE OIL

2 POUNDS BONELESS, SKINLESS CHICKEN THIGHS, CUT IN HALF

4 ANCHOVY FILLETS, CHOPPED

1 TABLESPOON MINCED GARLIC

ONE 28-OUNCE CAN CRUSHED TOMATOES IN PURÉE

1/2 CUP REDUCED-SODIUM CHICKEN BROTH

24 PITTED KALAMATA OLIVES, HALVED

3 TABLESPOONS NONPAREIL CAPERS (IN VINEGAR), RINSED

1/8 TEASPOON CRUSHED DRIED RED PEPPER FLAKES

Heat the olive oil in a Dutch oven over medium heat. Add the chicken in batches; sauté until browned, 4 to 5 minutes per side. Remove. Add the anchovy fillets and garlic; sauté until fragrant, 30 seconds to 1 minute. Add the tomatoes, chicken broth, olives, capers, and red pepper flakes; stir to blend. Return the chicken to the Dutch oven; reduce the heat to low. Cook, partially covered, until the chicken is fork-tender, about 40 minutes.

MAKE AHEAD Complete the entire recipe and simply reheat when ready.

SERVE WITH Pasta, garlic bread, and a tossed salad that has a bit of radicchio in it.

Recipes become classics for a reason. They are the proven favorites of generations of contented eaters. Chicken cacciatore is one of this select hall of fame. Also called hunter's stew, it takes simple ingredients and blends them in one simmering pot into something seriously gratifying.

Chicken Cacciatore

MAKES 6 SERVINGS

✳

3 TABLESPOONS OLIVE OIL

1 LARGE ONION, CHOPPED
(ABOUT 1½ CUPS)

2 LARGE CELERY STALKS,
CHOPPED (ABOUT 1 CUP)

2 LARGE GARLIC CLOVES,
CHOPPED (ABOUT
1 TABLESPOON)

8 OUNCES BABY PORTOBELLO
(CREMINI) MUSHROOMS, SLICED

12 BONELESS, SKINLESS
CHICKEN THIGHS, CUT IN HALF

¼ TEASPOON SALT

¼ TEASPOON FRESHLY
GROUND PEPPER

ONE 28-OUNCE CAN CRUSHED
TOMATOES IN PURÉE

½ CUP RED WINE

1 TABLESPOON CHOPPED
FRESH ROSEMARY

PINCH CRUSHED DRIED RED
PEPPER FLAKES

FRESHLY GRATED
PARMIGIANO-REGGIANO,
OPTIONAL

Heat 2 tablespoons of the olive oil in a Dutch oven over medium heat. Add the onion and celery: sauté until softened, 4 to 5 minutes. Add the garlic; sauté until fragrant, 30 seconds to 1 minute. Add the mushrooms; sauté until beginning to soften, 3 to 4 minutes. Remove.

Heat the remaining 1 tablespoon olive oil in the same Dutch oven. Sauté the chicken in batches, seasoned with the salt and pepper, until browned, 4 to 5 minutes per side. Return the mushroom mixture to the Dutch oven. Pour in the tomatoes and wine; add the rosemary and red pepper flakes. Stir to combine, scraping up any browned bits on the bottom of the pan. Bring just to a boil; reduce the heat to low and cook, uncovered, until the chicken is fork-tender, about 45 minutes. Serve with the Parmesan, if desired, on the side.

MAKE AHEAD Complete the recipe up to 2 days ahead of time and refrigerate, covered. Reheat when ready.

SERVE WITH Either pasta or polenta along with a tossed green salad.

Ragù is usually made with a variety of meats, but here dark-meat chicken is used instead for a lighter sauce.

Serve this with a pasta that catches and holds the sauce such as fusilli or rotini. Their spiral shape is perfect.

Chicken Ragù

MAKES 8 SERVINGS

✳

2 TABLESPOONS OLIVE OIL

2 MEDIUM CARROTS, PEELED AND CHOPPED (ABOUT 1 CUP)

2 MEDIUM CELERY STALKS, CHOPPED (ABOUT ^{2}/3 CUP)

1 LARGE ONION, CHOPPED (ABOUT 1^1/2 CUPS)

1 YELLOW BELL PEPPER, CHOPPED (ABOUT 1^1/2 CUPS)

2 OUNCES SALAMI, DICED (ABOUT ^{1}/2 CUP)

2 LARGE GARLIC CLOVES, CHOPPED (ABOUT 1 TABLESPOON)

8 OUNCES BABY PORTOBELLO (CREMINI) MUSHROOMS, SLICED

4 BONELESS, SKINLESS CHICKEN THIGHS, CUT IN ^{1}/2-INCH CUBES

ONE 28-OUNCE CAN CRUSHED TOMATOES IN PURÉE

^{1}/2 CUP RED WINE

^{1}/2 CUP REDUCED-SODIUM CHICKEN BROTH

2 TEASPOONS CHOPPED FRESH ROSEMARY

^{3}/4 TEASPOON CRUSHED FENNEL SEEDS

^{1}/8 TEASPOON CRUSHED DRIED RED PEPPER FLAKES

FRESHLY GRATED PARMIGIANO-REGGIANO, OPTIONAL

Heat the olive oil in a Dutch oven over medium heat. Add the carrots, celery, onion, and bell pepper; sauté until softened, 6 to 8 minutes. Stir in the salami and garlic; sauté until fragrant, 30 seconds to 1 minute. Add the mushrooms; sauté until softened, 5 to 7 minutes. Stir in the chicken; sauté until the chicken is no longer pink on the outside, 2 to 3 minutes. Add the tomatoes, red wine, chicken broth, rosemary, fennel seeds, and red pepper flakes. Bring just to a boil and reduce the heat to low; cook, uncovered, until thickened, stirring occasionally, about 45 minutes. Sprinkle with Parmesan, if desired.

MAKE AHEAD Make the whole recipe a day or two ahead of time and refrigerate, covered, until ready to serve, then bring to a simmer.

SERVE WITH Pasta plus slices of rustic, peasant-style bread on the side. A simple tossed romaine salad rounds out the menu.

In the fall, when the weather turns cool, I build a fire and simmer up a pot of this dynamite stew. Delivering major flavor with minimal effort, all this main dish needs is a good glass of wine and good company for a cozy evening of entertaining.

Portuguese Chicken and Sausage Stew

MAKES 6 SERVINGS

❋

2 TABLESPOONS OLIVE OIL

1 LARGE ONION, CHOPPED
(ABOUT 1½ CUPS)

4 LARGE GARLIC CLOVES,
CHOPPED (ABOUT
2 TABLESPOONS)

1 POUND PORTUGUESE CHORICE
OR LINGUIÇA, OR SPANISH-
STYLE SMOKED CHORIZO
(ABOUT 6 LINKS), CUT IN
THIRDS AND THEN EACH PIECE
HALVED LENGTHWISE

8 BONELESS, SKINLESS
CHICKEN THIGHS, CUT IN
THIRDS

½ TEASPOON SALT

¼ TEASPOON FRESHLY
GROUND PEPPER

ONE 28-OUNCE CAN CRUSHED
TOMATOES IN PURÉE

3/4 CUP RED WINE

1/8 TEASPOON
HOT PEPPER SAUCE

ONE 19-OUNCE CAN CANNELLINI
BEANS, DRAINED AND RINSED

¼ CUP CHOPPED FRESH BASIL

¼ CUP CHOPPED FRESH
PARSLEY

Heat 1 tablespoon of the olive oil in a Dutch oven over medium heat. Add the onion; sauté until softened, 4 to 5 minutes. Stir in the garlic and sauté until fragrant, 30 seconds to 1 minute. Remove to a medium bowl.

Add the remaining 1 tablespoon oil; when hot, add the sausage and sauté until browned, 3 to 4 minutes. Remove to the bowl.

Add the chicken in batches, seasoned with the salt and pepper; sauté until lightly browned, 4 to 5 minutes per side. Return the onion and sausage to the pan; add the tomatoes, red wine, and hot pepper sauce to the pot and stir to blend. Gently stir in the beans and reduce the heat to low; cook, partially covered, stirring occasionally, until the chicken is fork-tender, about 50 minutes. Stir in the basil and parsley; serve.

MAKE AHEAD Make the entire recipe ahead except for adding the basil and parsley. Refrigerate, covered, then reheat and add the basil and parsley.

SERVE WITH Start with a Caesar salad, then serve the stew with lots of bread.

eanuts (sometimes called groundnuts) are a common ingredient in West African cooking. Peanut butter is a common ingredient in American kitchens, and here it incorporates beautifully into the sauce, adding a velvety richness. Variations of this recipe also exist in southern American cookbooks, showing the influence of the African-American community on our cuisine.

Make this recipe as spicy as you wish, checking it at the end and adding extra cayenne, if desired.

African Chicken and Peanut Stew

MAKES 6 SERVINGS

❈

1 TABLESPOON PEANUT OR CANOLA OIL

1 LARGE ONION, CHOPPED (ABOUT 1¹/2 CUPS)

1 TEASPOON MINCED GINGER

ONE 14¹/2-OUNCE CAN DICED TOMATOES IN JUICE

¹/2 CUP PEANUT BUTTER

2 CUPS REDUCED-SODIUM CHICKEN BROTH

³/4 TEASPOON CAYENNE

¹/2 TEASPOON SALT

1 MEDIUM EGGPLANT (3/4 TO 1 POUND), CUT IN 1-INCH CUBES

6 OUNCES OKRA, TRIMMED AND CUT IN ¹/2-INCH PIECES (ABOUT 1¹/2 CUPS)

ONE 3¹/2- TO 4-POUND CHICKEN, CUT IN PIECES, WITH THE BREAST HALVES CUT IN HALF AGAIN ACROSS THE BONE IF LARGE

Heat the peanut oil in a Dutch oven over medium-low heat. Add the onion and sauté until softened, 6 to 8 minutes. Stir in the ginger; sauté for an additional minute. Stir in the tomatoes and their juice; simmer until slightly reduced, 3 to 4 minutes.

Stir the peanut butter with ¹/3 cup of the chicken broth in a medium bowl to thin; stir in the remaining broth along with the cayenne and salt. Add to the pot and stir to blend. Add the eggplant and okra; top with the chicken. Stir gently to mix. Bring to a simmer; reduce the heat to low and cook, partially covered, stirring occasionally, until the vegetables are tender and the chicken is no longer pink in the thickest portion when cut with a knife, about 1 hour.

MAKE AHEAD Complete the recipe and refrigerate, covered, until ready to reheat. Peanut butter works as a natural thickening agent, so you may need to thin the sauce with a bit of water. Don't overcook when reheating or the breasts will be dry.

SERVE WITH New potatoes and a tossed salad.

The British immediately come to mind when we think of colonialism in India. However, it was the Portuguese who spread their culture and cuisine throughout Goa, a western Indian state. In this Goan recipe, it is the vinegary taste—or *vindaloo*—that gives the dish its name. I've chosen tarragon vinegar, more commonly used in French cooking, as an excellent match to the other seasonings with its mildly anise flavor.

Chicken Vindaloo

MAKES 6 SERVINGS

❋

4 LARGE GARLIC CLOVES, CHOPPED (ABOUT 2 TABLESPOONS)

1 1/2 TABLESPOONS CHOPPED GINGER

2 TO 3 SERRANO CHILES, CHOPPED

1 TABLESPOON CANOLA OIL

1 LARGE RED ONION, CHOPPED (ABOUT 2 CUPS)

ONE 8-OUNCE CAN TOMATO SAUCE

2 TEASPOONS GROUND CORIANDER

1 TEASPOON GROUND CUMIN

1/2 TEASPOON SALT

ONE 5 1/2-OUNCE CAN COCONUT MILK (OR 3/4 CUP)

1/4 CUP TARRAGON WINE VINEGAR

9 BONELESS, SKINLESS CHICKEN THIGHS, CUT IN 2-INCH CUBES

1/3 CUP HEAVY CREAM

Chop the garlic, ginger, and serrano chiles together until finely minced; set aside. Heat the canola oil in a Dutch oven over medium-high heat; add the onion. Sauté until beginning to brown, 3 to 4 minutes. Add the minced garlic mixture; sauté until fragrant, 30 seconds to 1 minute. Stir in the tomato sauce, coriander, cumin, and salt; bring just to a simmer. Reduce the heat to low and cook until thickened, about 5 minutes. Add the coconut milk and vinegar; stir to blend.

Stir in the chicken; increase the heat to medium-low and bring to a simmer. Cook, partially covered, until the chicken is tender, about 35 minutes. Stir in the cream and cook for an additional 5 minutes, partially covered. Serve.

MAKE AHEAD The entire recipe can be prepared in advance and reheated.

SERVE WITH A heaping bowl of basmati rice to temper this spicy dish and with cooked baby peas.

When someone says mole, it's mole poblano that springs immediately to mind. Pueblan in origin, the wonderful sauce is rich with toasted chiles, nuts, and seeds, plus chocolate. It is best when made the day before, allowing all the ingredients to merge into a balanced whole.

Chicken Mole Poblano

MAKES 8 SERVINGS

❋

4 ANCHO CHILES

3 PASILLA CHILES

2 MULATO CHILES

$1/2$ CUP SLIVERED ALMONDS

3 TABLESPOONS SESAME SEEDS

$3^1/2$ TABLESPOONS CORN OIL

12 BONELESS, SKINLESS CHICKEN THIGHS

ONE $14^1/2$-OUNCE CAN DICED FIRE-ROASTED TOMATOES IN JUICE

1 MEDIUM ONION, CHOPPED (ABOUT $3/4$ CUP)

1 CORN TORTILLA, TORN

$1/3$ CUP RAISINS

1 LARGE GARLIC CLOVE, PEELED

$13/4$ TEASPOONS SALT

$1/2$ TEASPOON CINNAMON

$1/4$ TEASPOON GROUND ANISE

$1/4$ TEASPOON GROUND CORIANDER

PINCH GROUND CLOVES

1 OUNCE UNSWEETENED CHOCOLATE, CHOPPED

2 TO 3 TABLESPOONS SUGAR

Heat an empty Dutch oven over medium heat. Toast the chiles in batches until fragrant, about 2 minutes per side; remove. Toast the almonds until lightly browned, 2 to 3 minutes; remove. Toast the sesame seeds until lightly browned, stirring occasionally, 1 to 2 minutes; remove. Remove the pot from the heat. Remove the stems, membranes, and seeds from the chiles. Place the chiles in a medium bowl; cover with 1 quart boiling water. Soak for 40 minutes.

Meanwhile, using the same Dutch oven, heat 2 tablespoons of the corn oil over medium heat. Sauté the chicken in batches until browned, 4 to 5 minutes per side. Add enough water to cover; bring just to a boil. Reduce the heat to low and simmer until just cooked through, about 30 minutes. Remove the thighs. Strain and reserve the broth.

Drain the chiles and discard the soaking water; purée the chiles with the tomatoes, onion, tortilla, raisins, 1 cup of the reserved broth, and the garlic, in batches, in a blender.

Heat the remaining $1^1/2$ tablespoons oil in the Dutch oven over medium heat. Add the puréed chile mixture; stir in the salt, cinnamon, anise, coriander, and cloves. Cook, stirring frequently, for 5 minutes. Stir in the chopped chocolate and 2 cups of the reserved broth; reduce the heat to low and cook, stirring often, for 15 minutes. Stir in 2 tablespoons of the sugar; taste and add the remaining 1 tablespoon sugar, if necessary, to balance any bitterness.

Return the chicken to the pot; simmer, partially covered, to develop all the flavors, about 30 minutes.

MAKE AHEAD Instead of returning the thighs to the Dutch oven; arrange them in the bottom of a large, shallow baking dish and cover with the sauce. Refrigerate, covered. When ready to serve, heat the oven to 325°F. Cook, covered with aluminum foil, for 45 minutes.

SERVE WITH Rice and tortillas to soak up every last flavorful bite. Add guacamole as an appetizer, if you like, and a tossed salad with strips of jicama, orange slices, and a lime-honey salad dressing.

We tend to think of moles as being laced with chocolate, as in mole poblano, but there are many varieties. Derived from the Aztec word, *molli*, for sauce, Mexican moles are always cooked, but vary from the dark, brick-colored versions to the green stew featured here.

Pepitas are hulled pumpkin seeds and are pale sage green in color. I've called for the variety that comes already roasted. Should you find the raw variety, put them in a hot skillet and stir them until they begin to pop and they color a bit. Let them cool before using.

Chicken in Green Mole Sauce

MAKES 4 SERVINGS

✳

8 BONE-IN, SKINLESS
CHICKEN THIGHS

ONE 14-OUNCE CAN REDUCED-
SODIUM CHICKEN BROTH

1 MEDIUM ONION, QUARTERED

10 TOMATILLOS,
HUSKS REMOVED

3 JALAPEÑOS, STEMMED,
HALVED, AND SEEDED

2 LARGE GARLIC CLOVES,
PEELED

1 CUP ROASTED PEPITAS

4 ROMAINE LEAVES,
TORN IN PIECES

6 CILANTRO SPRIGS, PLUS
CILANTRO LEAVES

3/4 TEASPOON SALT

1/4 TEASPOON GROUND CUMIN

1/4 TEASPOON FRESHLY
GROUND PEPPER

1/8 TEASPOON CINNAMON

1 TABLESPOON OLIVE OIL

Place the chicken in a Dutch oven; add the chicken broth, onion, and 2 cups water. Bring just to a boil over medium heat. Reduce the heat to low and cook, uncovered, for 40 minutes, turning occasionally. Remove the chicken and set aside.

Add the tomatillos, jalapeños, and garlic to the broth and onion in the Dutch oven. Simmer for 15 minutes.

Finely grind the pepitas in a food processor fitted with a metal blade. Add 1 cup of the cooking broth from the pot and process to combine. Pour into a medium bowl. Remove the vegetables from the Dutch oven and place in the food processor, still fitted with the blade. Add the romaine, cilantro sprigs, salt, cumin, pepper, and cinnamon plus 1 cup of the cooking broth. Process to purée. Pour into a medium bowl. Remove the remaining broth from the Dutch oven and reserve.

Heat the olive oil in the same Dutch oven over medium heat. Add the pepita mixture and cook, stirring constantly, until very thick, 3 to 4 minutes. Stir in the vegetable mixture. Reduce the heat to medium-low and cook, stirring occasionally, uncovered, for 10 minutes. Add the chicken and cook for an additional 10 minutes, stirring occasionally, thinning the mixture with some of the reserved broth if it becomes too thick. Serve in the Dutch oven or remove the thighs to a platter and pour the mole sauce over the thighs. Garnish with cilantro leaves.

MAKE AHEAD Make the whole dish ahead and reheat when ready.

SERVE WITH Warm tortillas, rice, and a radish-topped green salad.

*T*he word "tagine" can mean either a type of pot or a style of cooking. Any tagine, or stew, meant for low heat and slow cooking, lends itself particularly well to thigh meat and this recipe is no exception.

Leaving the chicken on the bone adds body and extra flavor to the finished sauce. And what a sauce! Full of cumin, cinnamon, and ginger, it coats and complements the sweet carrots that are an integral part of this recipe.

Chicken and Carrot Tagine

MAKES 4 SERVINGS

✳

8 BONE-IN, SKINLESS
CHICKEN THIGHS

1 LARGE ONION, CHOPPED
(ABOUT 1 1/2 CUPS)

4 LARGE GARLIC CLOVES,
MINCED (ABOUT
2 TABLESPOONS)

2 TEASPOONS GROUND CUMIN

2 TEASPOONS CINNAMON

1 1/2 TEASPOONS
GROUND GINGER

1/2 TEASPOON SALT

PINCH CAYENNE

3 CUPS REDUCED-SODIUM
CHICKEN BROTH

1 TABLESPOON OLIVE OIL

1 POUND BABY CARROTS

1/2 CUP CHOPPED
FRESH PARSLEY

2 TABLESPOONS LEMON JUICE

1 TABLESPOON CHOPPED
FRESH MINT

Place the chicken in a Dutch oven; top with the onion and garlic. Sprinkle with the cumin, cinnamon, ginger, salt, and cayenne. Add the chicken broth and olive oil. Bring just to a boil over medium heat; reduce the heat to medium-low and cook, uncovered, for 45 minutes. Add the carrots, 1/4 cup of the parsley, and the lemon juice. Continue to cook until the carrots are tender, about 15 minutes. Remove the chicken and carrots with a slotted spoon to a platter. Increase the heat to high and boil to reduce the sauce by half, 6 to 8 minutes.

Return the chicken and carrots to the pot, reduce the heat to low, and cook briefly to rewarm, 2 to 3 minutes. Stir in the remaining 1/4 cup parsley; sprinkle with the mint and serve.

MAKE AHEAD Make the entire recipe up to adding the final parsley. After reheating, stir in the parsley as indicated and top with the mint.

SERVE WITH Cooked couscous.

Chickpeas, also called garbanzo beans, are part of the common thread of ingredients woven throughout Moroccan cooking, along with spices like ginger and cinnamon. What is amazing is the variety of recipes that result. Almonds add a lovely richness to the following tagine. While the nuts are typically cooked until soft, American palates prefer a bit of crunch, and the slivered almonds here retain some firmness that contrasts nicely with the softness of the chickpeas.

Chicken and Chickpea Tagine

✳

1 TABLESPOON OLIVE OIL

1 TABLESPOON SALTED BUTTER

1 LARGE ONION, CHOPPED
(ABOUT 1 1/2 CUPS)

1 TEASPOON GROUND GINGER

1/2 TEASPOON CINNAMON

8 BONE-IN, SKINLESS
CHICKEN THIGHS

3/4 TEASPOON FRESHLY
GROUND PEPPER

1/4 TEASPOON SALT

3/4 CUP SLIVERED ALMONDS

2 1/2 CUPS REDUCED-SODIUM
CHICKEN BROTH

1/8 TEASPOON SAFFRON
THREADS, CRUMBLED
(OR 1/8 TEASPOON TURMERIC)

ONE 15-OUNCE CAN GARBANZO
BEANS (CHICKPEAS), DRAINED
AND RINSED

1/4 CUP CHOPPED
FRESH PARSLEY

3 TABLESPOONS LEMON JUICE

2 TABLESPOONS
CHOPPED CILANTRO

Heat the olive oil and butter in a Dutch oven over medium heat. When sizzling, add the onion; sauté until softened, 4 to 5 minutes. Stir in the ginger and cinnamon; add the chicken, seasoned with the pepper and salt. Add the almonds and chicken broth; bring just to a boil. Stir in the saffron.

Reduce the heat to low and cook, partially covered, for 40 minutes. Remove the cover; stir in the garbanzo beans and cook until the liquid has reduced and thickened, about an additional 20 minutes. Stir in the parsley, lemon juice, and cilantro.

MAKE AHEAD Make the entire recipe ahead up to the point of adding the parsley, lemon juice, and cilantro. Refrigerate it, covered, until ready to serve. Reheat the mixture, covered, over low heat, stirring occasionally. When hot, stir in the parsley, lemon juice, and cilantro and serve.

SERVE WITH Diced fresh tomatoes and zucchini dressed with lemon juice and olive oil plus wedges of pita bread.

Whether you call them prunes or dried plums, adding these sweet morsels to a chicken stew is a touch of brilliance. They play against the savory ingredients and add a succulence to the finished dish that's hard to top.

Moroccan Chicken Tagine with Prunes

MAKES 6 SERVINGS

✳

2 TABLESPOONS OLIVE OIL

10 TO 12 BONELESS, SKINLESS CHICKEN THIGHS, CUT IN HALF

3/4 TEASPOON SALT

1/2 TEASPOON FRESHLY GROUND PEPPER

1 LARGE ONION, CHOPPED (ABOUT 1 1/2 CUPS)

3/4 TEASPOON CINNAMON

1/2 TEASPOON GROUND GINGER

1 1/2 CUPS BABY CARROTS

1 CUP FROZEN PEARL ONIONS, THAWED

1 TABLESPOON ORANGE BLOSSOM OR CLOVER HONEY

1 CUP DRIED PLUMS (PRUNES)

Heat the olive oil in a Dutch oven over medium heat. Add the chicken in batches, seasoned with the salt and pepper; sauté until lightly browned, 2 to 3 minutes per side. Remove. Add the onion; sauté for 1 minute. Add 1/4 cup water; reduce the heat to low. Cook for 5 minutes, scraping up any browned bits from the bottom of the pan. Stir in the cinnamon and ginger.

Return the chicken to the pan; add 1 1/2 cups water. Cook, partially covered, for 20 minutes. Add the carrots, onions, and honey; stir to combine and cook, partially covered, for an additional 20 minutes. Add the dried plums; stir to combine and cook, partially covered, for a final 20 minutes.

MAKE AHEAD Complete the recipe; refrigerate, covered. Reheat over low heat, stirring gently, when ready to serve.

SERVE WITH Couscous—the perfect accompaniment to almost any Moroccan stew.

Ras el hanout is a Moroccan spice blend. Like so many mixtures, it varies in its final content depending on the preferences of the person combining the ingredients. It can be ordered through the Internet or found in North African specialty stores. For an acceptable alternative, feel free to blend curry powder, which shares many spices in common with ras el hanout, along with cumin and cinnamon.

Chicken and Sweet Potato Tagine

MAKES 4 SERVINGS

※

8 BONE-IN, SKINLESS CHICKEN THIGHS

1 LARGE ONION, CHOPPED (ABOUT 1½ CUPS)

3 MEDIUM ROMA TOMATOES, CHOPPED (ABOUT 1 CUP)

1 TEASPOON GROUND GINGER

1 TEASPOON RAS EL HANOUT (OR ½ TEASPOON MILD CURRY POWDER, ½ TEASPOON GROUND CUMIN, AND ¼ TEASPOON CINNAMON)

3/4 TEASPOON SALT

½ TEASPOON FRESHLY GROUND PEPPER

ONE 14-OUNCE CAN REDUCED-SODIUM CHICKEN BROTH

½ CUP GOLDEN RAISINS

2 TABLESPOONS MILD HONEY

3 MEDIUM SWEET POTATOES, YAMS, OR GARNET YAMS (ABOUT 1½ POUNDS), PEELED AND CUT IN 1-INCH SLICES

Place the chicken in the bottom of a Dutch oven; top with the onion and tomatoes. Sprinkle with the ginger, ras el hanout, salt, and pepper. Add the chicken broth and gently stir to blend. Bring just to a boil over medium heat; reduce the heat to medium-low and cook, uncovered, for 40 minutes, stirring occasionally.

Add the raisins and honey; stir to blend. Add the sweet potatoes and push them into the mixture so that they are covered with broth. Continue to cook, uncovered, until the potatoes are just tender, about 30 minutes.

Remove the chicken and potatoes to a platter and increase the heat to high. Boil until reduced by half, 6 to 8 minutes. Return the chicken and potatoes to the pot; reduce the heat to low and cook briefly to rewarm, 2 to 3 minutes.

MAKE AHEAD Complete the entire recipe and refrigerate, covered, until ready to reheat. Reheat this recipe in a 350°F oven, covered, until hot, 30 to 40 minutes. Reheating in the oven will warm the mixture more evenly and eliminate any stirring that might break up the sweet potatoes.

SERVE WITH A tossed salad topped with pine nuts and pita bread.

*W*alnuts and chicken are a frequent combination—common in southern France, Turkey, and, in this case, Iran. The Iranians provide an extra zing by adding pomegranates. Some versions call for pomegranate molasses, a thickly concentrated essence, but juice is easier to find and works just as well when reduced.

Pomegranate and Walnut Stew

MAKES 4 SERVINGS

❋

2 CUPS CHOPPED WALNUTS

2 TABLESPOONS OLIVE OIL

4 BONE-IN, SKIN-ON CHICKEN THIGHS

2 BONE-IN, SKIN-ON CHICKEN BREAST HALVES, CUT IN HALF ACROSS THE BONE IF LARGE

1/2 TEASPOON SALT

1/4 TEASPOON FRESHLY GROUND PEPPER

1 LARGE ONION, CHOPPED (ABOUT 1 1/2 CUPS)

2 TABLESPOONS SUGAR

2 CUPS POMEGRANATE JUICE

2 TABLESPOONS LEMON JUICE

1/4 TEASPOON CINNAMON

Toast the walnuts in a large, dry skillet over medium-high heat, stirring occasionally, until the nuts turn oily and fragrant and begin to brown, 3 to 5 minutes. Remove and let cool.

Add the olive oil to the same skillet; sauté the chicken in batches, seasoned with the salt and pepper, until browned, 3 to 4 minutes per side. Remove to a plate. Pour off all but 2 tablespoons of the fat; add the onion and sauté until lightly browned, 4 to 5 minutes. Stir in the sugar; continue to cook, stirring often, until a rich brown, 3 to 4 minutes. Add the pomegranate juice, lemon juice, and cinnamon; boil until reduced by one-third, 3 to 5 minutes.

Meanwhile, grind the nuts in a food processor fitted with a metal blade until finely ground but not a paste. Stir the nuts into the reduced pomegranate mixture. Return the chicken to the skillet; turn to coat. Cook, partially covered, turning once, until the chicken is no longer pink in the thickest portion when cut with a knife, 35 to 45 minutes.

MAKE AHEAD Toast the walnuts and assemble all the ingredients before preparing. If the full recipe is completed in advance, add a bit of water to the sauce before reheating, covered, in a 350°F oven for 20 to 30 minutes. If the sauce looks curdled, whisk a bit of hot water into the sauce before serving.

SERVE WITH Basmati rice, green beans, and pita bread.

I prepared this dish for a Divali party at my friend Raghavan's home, where grown-ups and children gathered for an eclectic potluck to celebrate the Indian festival of lights. While this stew would typically be served with the chicken thighs on the bone, you may wish to remove the bones after cooking, as I did for the party, for ease of serving and eating. I've also made the dal choices a bit more mainstream and accessible, using yellow split peas (*chana dal*) and readily available green split peas instead of split pigeon peas and split, dried lima beans.

MAKES 8 SERVINGS

❋

2 TABLESPOONS GHEE
(CLARIFIED SALTED BUTTER) OR
CANOLA OIL

1 LARGE RED ONION, HALVED
LENGTHWISE AND SLICED

8 BONE-IN, SKINLESS
CHICKEN THIGHS

2 TEASPOONS SALT

1/4 TEASPOON FRESHLY
GROUND PEPPER

1/2 CUP YELLOW SPLIT PEAS

1/2 CUP GREEN SPLIT PEAS

2 SERRANO CHILES, SLICED

2 BAY LEAVES

1 TEASPOON GARAM MASALA

1/4 TEASPOON CINNAMON

1/4 TEASPOON GROUND CLOVES

1/4 TEASPOON TURMERIC

2 CUPS PEELED, SEEDED, AND
DICED DELICATA OR
BUTTERNUT SQUASH

Chicken with Split Peas

Heat the ghee in a Dutch oven over medium heat. Add the onion; sauté until softened and lightly browned, 6 to 8 minutes. Remove half the onion and set aside. Add the chicken, seasoned with 1/2 teaspoon of the salt and the pepper; sauté until lightly browned, 2 to 3 minutes per side. Add 3 cups water, the yellow and green split peas, serrano chiles, bay leaves, garam masala, cinnamon, cloves, turmeric, and remaining 1 1/2 teaspoons salt; stir to blend. Bring just to a boil; reduce the heat to low and cook, partially covered, until the split peas are tender to the bite and the chicken is no longer pink in the thickest portion when cut with a knife, about 45 minutes.

Add the squash, tomatoes with their juice, and the spinach; stir to blend. Return to a simmer; cook, partially covered, until the squash is tender, 25 to 30 minutes. Stir in the lime zest, lime juice, and reserved onion. Remove the bay leaves. (If desired, remove the chicken and cut the meat from the bone. Return the meat to the pot and serve.)

MAKE AHEAD Make the recipe completely except for adding the lime zest and juice. Refrigerate it, covered, until just before serving and then reheat. Add the lime zest and juice and stir to blend.

SERVE WITH A bowl of basmati rice and some naan for a satisfying meal.

ONE 14$\frac{1}{2}$-OUNCE CAN DICED TOMATOES IN JUICE

ONE 9-OUNCE PACKAGE FROZEN CHOPPED SPINACH, THAWED

1 TEASPOON GRATED LIME ZEST

2 TABLESPOONS LIME JUICE

$\mathcal{I}$f you do a Web search of Bohemia, you'll find references to the Austro-Hungarian Empire, Czechoslovakia, and Prague, giving a sense of the centuries of history behind this country-that-was. Bohemian stew, full of plump chicken pieces and cabbage, accented with caraway and cream, is worthy of its rich heritage.

Bohemian Chicken Stew

MAKES 4 SERVINGS

❋

2 TABLESPOONS CANOLA OIL

4 BONE-IN, SKIN-ON
CHICKEN THIGHS

2 BONE-IN, SKIN-ON CHICKEN
BREAST HALVES

1/2 TEASPOON SALT

1/4 TEASPOON FRESHLY
GROUND PEPPER

1 LARGE ONION, CHOPPED
(ABOUT 1 1/2 CUPS)

1 TABLESPOON SUGAR

3 TABLESPOONS ALL-PURPOSE
FLOUR

1 1/2 TEASPOONS SWEET
PAPRIKA, PREFERABLY
HUNGARIAN

1/8 TEASPOON GROUND CLOVES

1/2 CUP APPLE CIDER

ONE 14-OUNCE CAN REDUCED-
SODIUM CHICKEN BROTH

3 LARGE CELERY STALKS, CUT IN
1-INCH PIECES

2 LARGE CARROTS, PEELED,
HALVED LENGTHWISE, AND CUT
IN 1-INCH PIECES

3/4 TEASPOON CARAWAY SEEDS

1/2 SMALL HEAD
GREEN CABBAGE, CUT IN
2 × 1-INCH SHREDS

1/4 CUP CRÈME FRAÎCHE

Heat the canola oil in a Dutch oven over medium heat. Add the chicken in batches, seasoned with the salt and pepper; sauté until browned, 4 to 5 minutes per side. Remove.

Drain all but 2 tablespoons of fat from the pan; add the onion and sauté for 2 minutes, stirring often and scraping the browned bits from the bottom to prevent scorching. Add the sugar; sauté for an additional 1 minute.

Reduce the heat to medium-low and stir in the flour; cook for 2 minutes, stirring often. Stir in the paprika and cloves until well combined; stir in the apple cider until all the flour is blended. Slowly stir in the chicken broth.

Return the chicken to the pot; add the celery, carrots, and caraway seeds. Bring just to a simmer; partially cover and cook for 10 minutes.

Stir in the cabbage and reduce the heat to low; cook, partially covered, for an additional 15 minutes.

Remove the cover and cook, stirring occasionally, until the chicken is no longer pink when cut with a knife in the thickest portion, about 15 additional minutes. Stir in the crème fraîche until well blended and cook to heat through, 1 to 2 minutes.

MAKE AHEAD Complete the recipe up to adding the crème fraîche and refrigerate, covered. When ready to serve, reheat the stew gently over low heat until just warmed through. Add the crème fraîche and cook for an additional 1 to 2 minutes as directed.

SERVE WITH Spaetzle, egg noodles, or boiled new potatoes and thick slices of rye bread. Beer, cider, or Riesling is a sound beverage choice.

hunks of moist chicken team up with bits of bacon, root vegetables, and dill to send irresistible aromas into every cranny of your home. If that's not enough, the stew is topped with plump mounds of caraway-studded dumplings, providing just the right vehicle to convey all the creamy sauce from bowl to mouth.

German Chicken Stew with Caraway Dumplings

MAKES 4 SERVINGS

✳

2 TABLESPOONS CANOLA OIL

2 BACON SLICES, CUT IN
$1/4$-INCH STRIPS

8 BONELESS, SKINLESS CHICKEN
THIGHS, CUT IN HALF

$1/2$ TEASPOON SALT

$1/4$ TEASPOON FRESHLY GROUND
PEPPER

3 TABLESPOONS ALL-PURPOSE
FLOUR

3 CUPS REDUCED-SODIUM
CHICKEN BROTH

1 TABLESPOON DIJON MUSTARD

1 MEDIUM CELERY ROOT,
PEELED AND CUT IN $3/4$-INCH
CUBES (ABOUT 4 CUPS)

3 MEDIUM CARROTS, PEELED,
HALVED LENGTHWISE, AND CUT
IN $3/4$-INCH PIECES

$1^1/2$ CUPS FROZEN PEARL
ONIONS, THAWED

2 TABLESPOONS CHOPPED
FRESH DILL WEED
(OR 2 TEASPOONS DRIED
DILL WEED)

1 LARGE EGG

$1/4$ CUP MILK

Heat 1 tablespoon of the canola oil in a Dutch oven over medium-high heat. Add the bacon strips and sauté until lightly browned, about 2 minutes. Remove with a slotted spoon.

Season the chicken with the salt and pepper and add half to the pot, skin side down. Sauté until browned, 3 to 4 minutes. Turn and brown the other side, 3 to 4 minutes; remove. Repeat with the remaining chicken. Pour off all but 2 tablespoons of the fat; stir in the all-purpose flour and cook for 1 minute, stirring constantly. Whisk in the chicken broth and mustard until well blended. Return the chicken and bacon to the pan; add the celery root, carrots, and pearl onions. Bring just to a boil and reduce the heat to low. Cook, uncovered, for 40 minutes; stir in the dill.

Meanwhile, whisk the egg and the remaining 1 tablespoon canola oil together in a small bowl. Whisk in the milk and parsley. Put the self-rising flour into a medium bowl; stir in the caraway seeds and make a well in the center. Stir in the egg mixture until blended into a dough.

After the chicken has cooked for 40 minutes, dip a tablespoon into the hot liquid and then into the dough. Drop the spoonful of dough into the Dutch oven; continue with the rest of the dough, about 8 spoonfuls in all. Cook, covered, until the dumplings are fluffy, 20 minutes. Serve in shallow bowls.

MAKE AHEAD Prepare the recipe through cooking the chicken and vegetables for 40 minutes and then refrigerate, covered. When ready, reheat the chicken, add the dill, and make the dumpling dough. Proceed as directed.

SERVE WITH A salad of mixed greens that also contains bits of red cabbage.

1¹/₂ TABLESPOONS CHOPPED
FRESH PARSLEY

1 CUP PLUS 2 TABLESPOONS
SELF-RISING FLOUR, PREFERABLY
WHITE LILY

4 TEASPOONS CARAWAY SEEDS

4 Braises

*B*raising and stewing are similar techniques, but braising uses less liquid and the food is gently cooked over time in a covered container. Here, the balsamic vinegar cooks with the chicken first so that its distinctively sweet-sour taste and darker color permeate the meat, before small quantities of wine and broth are added.

Balsamic Braised Chicken

MAKES 6 SERVINGS

1 TABLESPOON OLIVE OIL

12 BONE-IN, SKIN-ON CHICKEN THIGHS

1/2 TEASPOON SALT

1/4 TEASPOON FRESHLY GROUND PEPPER

2 LARGE GARLIC CLOVES, MINCED (ABOUT 1 TABLESPOON)

2 1/2 TEASPOONS CHOPPED FRESH ROSEMARY

1 1/2 TEASPOONS CHOPPED FRESH SAGE

1/3 CUP BALSAMIC VINEGAR

1/2 CUP RED WINE

1/2 CUP REDUCED-SODIUM CHICKEN BROTH

1 CUP FROZEN PEARL ONIONS, THAWED

3 SMALL ZUCCHINI, CUT IN 1/2-INCH CHUNKS

Heat the olive oil in a Dutch oven over medium-high heat. Add the chicken thighs, seasoned with the salt and pepper; sauté until browned on both sides, 4 to 5 minutes per side. Sprinkle with the garlic, 2 teaspoons of the rosemary, and 1 teaspoon of the sage; turn.

Pour in the balsamic vinegar; reduce the heat to low. Cook, covered, for 5 minutes on one side; turn and cook, covered, for an additional 5 minutes on the other side. Add the red wine, chicken broth, and pearl onions. Simmer, covered, for 25 minutes. Turn the chicken; add the zucchini. Cook until the zucchini is just tender and the chicken is no longer pink when cut with a knife in the thickest portion, about 15 minutes.

Remove the chicken and vegetables to a platter with a slotted spoon; cover to keep warm. Skim the surface fat off the cooking liquid; add the remaining 1/2 teaspoon each rosemary and sage. Increase the heat to high and boil until reduced by about one-third and the vinegar in the sauce tastes mellow, 4 to 5 minutes. Return the chicken to the pot or pour the sauce over the chicken on the platter.   *(continued)*

MAKE AHEAD Prepare the recipe until the chicken is cooked through and refrigerate, covered. When ready, re-heat gently and proceed as directed.

SERVE WITH Lots of bread and a simple salad dressed with extra virgin olive oil.

While this dish is traditionally made with chicken pieces split into smaller portions with a Chinese cleaver, chicken-wing drumettes make this braised appetizer as easy as it is delicious.

For an interesting variation, use chicken thighs and cut the meat in slivers after cooking. Place the slivered chicken on top of lettuce or baby bok choy and drizzle with the braising liquid for a tasty and unusual warm chicken salad.

Soy-Braised Chicken Wings

MAKES 8 TO 10 APPETIZER SERVINGS, OR 4 MAIN-COURSE SERVINGS

❋

1/2 CUP SOY SAUCE, PREFERABLY CHINESE OR KIKKOMAN

3 TABLESPOONS CHOPPED GINGER

2 TABLESPOONS HOISIN SAUCE

2 TABLESPOONS RICE WINE (OR SHERRY)

2 TABLESPOONS PACKED LIGHT BROWN SUGAR

2 LARGE GARLIC CLOVES, MINCED (ABOUT 1 TABLESPOON)

1 TABLESPOON RED WINE VINEGAR

1/2 TEASPOON FIVE-SPICE POWDER

3 POUNDS CHICKEN-WING DRUMETTES (OR 3 POUNDS CHICKEN WINGS, TIPS REMOVED AND CUT IN 2 PIECES AT THE JOINT)

2 TEASPOONS TOASTED SESAME OIL

Mix the soy sauce, ginger, hoisin sauce, rice wine, brown sugar, garlic, vinegar, and five-spice powder together in a Dutch oven. Add the chicken and turn to coat. Marinate for 30 minutes at room temperature, stirring occasionally. Add 1 cup water; bring just to a boil over medium heat. Reduce the heat to low and simmer for 40 minutes, covered, stirring once halfway through. Remove from the heat and stir in the sesame oil. Let rest, covered, for an additional 20 minutes. Remove from the braising liquid with a slotted spoon and serve.

MAKE AHEAD Refrigerate the chicken in the braising liquid. Reheat in the liquid over low heat and serve as directed.

SERVE WITH While I've suggested this as an appetizer rather than a main course, these drumettes could be served with some of their braising liquid over rice and some steamed broccoli.

I love the Spanish tradition of adding their glorious Serrano ham as a flavoring agent to other recipes. Often chopped and added with onion, bell pepper, and tomato, here the chopped ham is stuffed under the chicken's skin for an even more pronounced effect.

In the winter, when fresh tomatoes are less than lovely, substitute a 14½-ounce can of diced tomatoes and their juice.

MAKES 4 SERVINGS

✳

ONE 3½- TO 4-POUND CHICKEN, QUARTERED AND WINGS REMOVED (RESERVE THE WINGS FOR ANOTHER USE)

3 OUNCES SERRANO HAM, PROSCIUTTO, OR BAYONNE HAM, CUT IN ½-INCH DICE (ABOUT ¾ CUP)

¼ TEASPOON FRESHLY GROUND PEPPER

1 TABLESPOON OLIVE OIL

1 LARGE ONION, CHOPPED (ABOUT 1½ CUPS)

½ RED BELL PEPPER, CHOPPED (ABOUT ¾ CUP)

1 LARGE GARLIC CLOVE, CHOPPED (ABOUT 1½ TEASPOONS)

3 MEDIUM TOMATOES (ABOUT 1 POUND), CHOPPED (ABOUT 2 CUPS)

⅛ TEASPOON SALT

¼ CUP COGNAC (OR BRANDY)

Chicken with Serrano Ham

To loosen the skin on the chicken pieces, work from one side on the breast pieces, leaving the skin attached to a small portion of the flesh on the other side; loosen the skin around the thigh and the upper portion of the drumstick on the leg portions. Stuff the ham under the skin, flattening as necessary to eliminate lumps and to spread more evenly. Season with ⅛ teaspoon of the pepper.

Heat the olive oil in a large skillet over medium-high heat. Add the chicken, skin side down; sauté until deeply browned, about 5 minutes. Turn and brown the other side, 4 to 5 minutes. Remove. Add the onion and bell pepper; sauté until softened, 3 to 4 minutes. Add the garlic and sauté until fragrant, 30 seconds to 1 minute. Add the tomatoes, salt, and remaining ⅛ teaspoon pepper. Stir to blend and cook until the tomatoes have softened and begun to yield their juice, 3 to 4 minutes.

Return the chicken to the skillet and pour the Cognac over all. Immediately light with a match to flame. When the flame disappears, reduce the heat to low and cook, covered, turning once during cooking, until the chicken is no longer pink when cut with a knife in the thickest portion, 35 to 40 minutes.

MAKE AHEAD Prepare the entire recipe ahead and reheat when ready.

SERVE WITH Saffron rice and a salad tossed with sherry vinegar and extra virgin olive oil.

In late summer, when the markets overflow with peppers, eggplant, and zucchini, my mouth begins to water for ratatouille, and my thoughts turn to my house in Provence. I've discovered that the Spanish make a similar version of my French standby, only with chicken, making it perfect for effortless entertaining. I couldn't resist adding basil at the end to spark the final taste, bringing the full effect closer to what tastes like home to me.

Spanish Chicken with Ratatouille Vegetables

MAKES 4 SERVINGS

※

2 TABLESPOONS OLIVE OIL

4 BONE-IN, SKIN-ON
CHICKEN THIGHS

2 BONE-IN, SKIN-ON CHICKEN
BREAST HALVES, CUT IN HALF
ACROSS THE BONE

1 TEASPOON SALT

$1/4$ TEASPOON FRESHLY
GROUND PEPPER

1 LARGE ONION, CHOPPED
(ABOUT $1^1/2$ CUPS)

2 LARGE GARLIC CLOVES,
MINCED (ABOUT 1 TABLESPOON)

1 RED OR YELLOW BELL PEPPER,
CUT IN 1-INCH PIECES

1 GREEN BELL PEPPER, CUT IN
1-INCH PIECES

1 MEDIUM-SMALL EGGPLANT
(ABOUT $3/4$ POUND), CUT IN
1-INCH CHUNKS

2 MEDIUM ZUCCHINI, HALVED
LENGTHWISE AND CUT IN
1-INCH PIECES

Heat the olive oil in a Dutch oven over medium heat. Add the chicken in batches, seasoned with $1/4$ teaspoon of the salt and $1/8$ teaspoon of the pepper; sauté until golden brown, 3 to 4 minutes per side. Remove. Add the onion; sauté until softened, 4 to 5 minutes. Stir in the garlic; sauté until fragrant, 30 seconds to 1 minute. Stir in the bell peppers, then the eggplant; sauté until beginning to soften, about 4 minutes. Stir in the zucchini; sauté for an additional 1 minute.

Add the tomatoes, red wine, thyme, remaining $3/4$ teaspoon salt, and remaining $1/8$ teaspoon pepper; stir to blend. Return the chicken to the Dutch oven, pushing the pieces into the vegetable mixture. Reduce the heat to low; cook, covered, until the chicken is no longer pink in the thickest portion when cut with a knife, 45 to 50 minutes. Stir in the basil and serve immediately.

Prepare the entire recipe except for adding the basil. When ready to serve, rewarm gently over medium-low heat, partially covered, until piping hot, 25 to 30 minutes. Stir in the basil and serve.

SERVE WITH Triangles of polenta, dusted with Parmesan. Fill in with a simple salad tossed with a citrus vinaigrette.

3 TO 4 MEDIUM TOMATOES (ABOUT 1 POUND), COARSELY CHOPPED (ABOUT 2 CUPS)

1/3 CUP RED WINE

1/2 TEASPOON DRIED THYME

1/4 CUP CHOPPED FRESH BASIL

The idea of cooking *al* or *en chilindrón*—with peppers—comes from Aragon, the area that leads to the mountainous Basque region. The combination of red peppers, both sweet bell and spicy jalapeño, cooked with tomatoes and ham, is reminiscent of the Basque chicken recipe in my book *Bistro Chicken*.

MAKES 6 SERVINGS

✳

3 TABLESPOONS OLIVE OIL

9 BONELESS, SKINLESS
CHICKEN THIGHS, CUT IN HALF

3/4 TEASPOON SALT

1/4 TEASPOON FRESHLY
GROUND PEPPER

1 LARGE ONION, CHOPPED
(ABOUT 1 1/2 CUPS)

1 LARGE GARLIC CLOVE,
CHOPPED (ABOUT
1 1/2 TEASPOONS)

3 RED BELL PEPPERS, CUT IN
2 × 1/4-INCH STRIPS

1 RED JALAPEÑO, CHOPPED
(SEEDED AND MEMBRANES
REMOVED, IF DESIRED)

2 OUNCES THINLY SLICED
SERRANO HAM OR PROSCIUTTO,
CUT IN 1/2-INCH PIECES
(ABOUT 1/2 CUP)

ONE 14 1/2-OUNCE CAN DICED
TOMATOES IN JUICE

Pollo al Chilindrón

(Chicken with Peppers)

Heat 2 tablespoons of the olive oil in a Dutch oven over medium-high heat. Sauté the chicken in batches, seasoned with the salt and pepper, until browned, 3 to 4 minutes per side; remove. Add the remaining 1 tablespoon olive oil; add the onion. Reduce the heat to medium-low; sauté the onion until softened, 6 to 8 minutes. Add the garlic; sauté until fragrant, 30 seconds to 1 minute. Add the red bell peppers and jalapeño; sauté until beginning to soften, about 4 minutes. Add the Serrano ham; stir to combine. Sauté until the peppers are tender, 3 to 4 minutes. Stir in the tomatoes and their juice.

Return the chicken to the pan; stir to combine. Bring just to a boil; reduce the heat to low and simmer, covered, for 40 minutes. Remove the cover; stir and simmer for an additional 15 minutes to reduce and concentrate the released vegetable juices.

MAKE AHEAD Make the entire recipe ahead of time. Refrigerate, covered, until ready to reheat.

SERVE WITH Plenty of rice and a salad of mixed greens topped with toasted walnuts.

*S*ugar snap peas, while not traditional, work ever so well in this simply prepared recipe from Portugal. They are available fresh all year round, unlike regular shelling peas, and are certainly speedier to prepare. Simply remove any tough outer strings along the edges and they are ready to use.

MAKES 4 SERVINGS

❋

2 TABLESPOONS OLIVE OIL

3 BACON SLICES, DICED

1 LARGE ONION, CHOPPED
(ABOUT 1½ CUPS)

4 BONE-IN, SKIN-ON
CHICKEN THIGHS

2 BONE-IN, SKIN-ON
CHICKEN BREAST HALVES

½ TEASPOON SALT

¼ TEASPOON FRESHLY
GROUND PEPPER

1 CUP REDUCED-SODIUM
CHICKEN BROTH

⅓ CUP DRY PORTUGUESE
MADEIRA OR RED WINE

1 TABLESPOON TOMATO PASTE

8 OUNCES SUGAR SNAP PEAS
(2½ TO 3 CUPS)

Frango com Ervilhas

(Portuguese Chicken with Peas)

Heat 1 tablespoon of the olive oil in a Dutch oven over medium heat. Add the bacon and sauté, stirring frequently, until it just begins to brown, 2 to 3 minutes. Add the onion and sauté until softened and beginning to brown, 4 to 5 minutes. Remove to a bowl. Add the remaining 1 tablespoon olive oil. Add the chicken in batches, seasoned with the salt and pepper; sauté until browned, 4 to 5 minutes per side. Add the chicken broth, Madeira, tomato paste, and bacon-and-onion mixture. Stir to blend.

Bring just to a boil; reduce the heat to low and cook, covered, turning occasionally, until the chicken is no longer pink in the thickest portion when cut with a knife, 35 to 45 minutes. Add the sugar snap peas; stir to combine. Cook, covered, until the peas turn bright green, about 2 minutes.

MAKE AHEAD Prepare the recipe up to adding the sugar snap peas; refrigerate, covered. When ready, gently reheat, then add the sugar snaps.

SERVE WITH Roasted potatoes or hash browns. Add a crisp salad and crusty bread.

You'll find the flavors truly intoxicating in this Italian recipe for drunken chicken. Unlike the Mexican version where the poultry is braised in beer, here the chicken is a two-fisted drinker, reveling in both white and red wine.

MAKES 4 SERVINGS

❊

3 TABLESPOONS OLIVE OIL

1/2 CUP CHOPPED SHALLOTS

2 LARGE GARLIC
CLOVES, CHOPPED
(ABOUT 1 TABLESPOON)

5 TEASPOONS MINCED
FRESH ROSEMARY

1/2 TEASPOON DRIED
THYME

8 OUNCES BABY PORTOBELLO
(CREMINI) MUSHROOMS, SLICED

8 BONE-IN, SKINLESS
CHICKEN THIGHS

1/2 TEASPOON SALT

1/4 TEASPOON FRESHLY
GROUND PEPPER

1 CUP WHITE WINE

1/4 CUP DRIED CURRANTS

PINCH CRUSHED DRIED RED
PEPPER FLAKES

1 CUP RED WINE

Pollo Ubriaco (Drunken Chicken)

Heat 2 tablespoons of the olive oil in a large skillet over medium heat. Add the shallots; sauté for 2 minutes. Add the garlic, rosemary, and thyme; sauté until fragrant, 30 seconds to 1 minute. Add the mushrooms; sauté until softened, 4 to 5 minutes; remove.

Add the remaining 1 tablespoon olive oil; increase the heat to medium-high. Add the chicken in batches, seasoned with the salt and pepper; sauté until browned, 4 to 5 minutes per side. Return the mushroom mixture to the skillet; pour in the white wine. Reduce the heat to low; cook, uncovered, for 5 minutes. Add the currants and red pepper flakes; stir gently and turn the chicken. Cook, covered, for 15 minutes. Turn the chicken again and add the red wine. Cook, covered, until the chicken is fork-tender and no longer pink in the thickest portion when cut with a knife, about an additional 20 minutes.

Remove the chicken; increase the heat to high and boil to reduce the sauce slightly, 3 to 4 minutes. Pour over the chicken and serve.

MAKE AHEAD Complete the recipe up to reducing the sauce. Reheat the chicken and sauce over low heat, and then remove the chicken to reduce the sauce.

SERVE WITH A green salad with a balsamic vinaigrette, green beans, and a crunchy baguette.

Who knew chicken was such a party animal? Here the tipple of choice is beer, lubricating our tipsy bird in a most efficacious way while blending deliciously with the cumin and ancho seasonings.

Mexican Beer-Braised Chicken (Drunken Chicken)

MAKES 4 SERVINGS

❋

1/2 CUP CORNMEAL

2 TEASPOONS ANCHO CHILE POWDER

2 TEASPOONS GROUND CUMIN

3/4 TEASPOON SALT

ONE 3 1/2- TO 4-POUND CHICKEN, CUT IN PIECES

1 TABLESPOON OLIVE OIL

1 LARGE ONION, CHOPPED (ABOUT 1 1/2 CUPS)

1 GREEN BELL PEPPER, CHOPPED (ABOUT 1 1/2 CUPS)

1 JALAPEÑO, CHOPPED

1 LARGE GARLIC CLOVE, CHOPPED (ABOUT 1 1/2 TEASPOONS)

ONE 11- OR 12-OUNCE BOTTLE OR CAN OF BEER, SUCH AS MEXICAN CORONA

1 CUP CHOPPED TOMATO

1/2 CUP REDUCED-SODIUM CHICKEN BROTH

1 TABLESPOON LIME JUICE

1 TABLESPOON PACKED LIGHT BROWN SUGAR

1 SMALL ZUCCHINI, CUT IN 1/2-INCH SLICES

1 SMALL YELLOW SQUASH, CUT IN 1/2-INCH SLICES

Combine the cornmeal, ancho chile powder, cumin, and 1/2 teaspoon of the salt in a shallow bowl; mix well. Reserve 1 tablespoon of the mixture; dredge the chicken pieces on both sides in the remaining cornmeal mixture.

Heat the olive oil in a Dutch oven over medium-high heat; sauté the chicken in batches until browned, 3 to 4 minutes per side. Remove and set aside. Add the onion; sauté for 2 minutes. Add the bell pepper; sauté for 2 minutes. Add the jalapeño and garlic; sauté until fragrant, 30 seconds to 1 minute. Return the chicken to the Dutch oven; add the beer, tomato, chicken broth, lime juice, brown sugar, and remaining 1/4 teaspoon salt. Stir to blend. Bring just to a boil; reduce the heat to low and cook, covered, for 20 minutes. Stir in the reserved cornmeal mixture, blending well; stir in the zucchini and yellow squash. Cook, covered, until the chicken is no longer pink in the thickest portion when cut with a knife, about an additional 20 minutes.

MAKE AHEAD Complete the recipe and refrigerate, covered. Before serving, gently reheat until just warmed through.

SERVE WITH Tortillas, more beer, and an orange and jicama salad.

While the Germans would dispute it, Belgium may very well be the home of the world's best beer. I know my Belgian cousin, Joseph, would certainly agree. It's no surprise, then, that beer-braised chicken is the star of this Belgian recipe, accented with tart-sweet Granny Smith apples.

Using two chicken breasts and four thighs is a heartier option than using a cut-up bird, with more meat on the thighs than there would be on drumsticks.

Chicken with Beer and Apples

MAKES 4 SERVINGS

*

2 TABLESPOONS SALTED BUTTER

2 GRANNY SMITH APPLES, CORED AND CUT IN 3/4-INCH WEDGES

1/4 CUP ALL-PURPOSE FLOUR

1 TEASPOON SALT

1/4 TEASPOON FRESHLY GROUND PEPPER

1/8 TEASPOON GROUND NUTMEG

4 BONE-IN, SKIN-ON CHICKEN THIGHS

2 BONE-IN, SKIN-ON CHICKEN BREAST HALVES

1 TABLESPOON CANOLA OIL

1 MEDIUM ONION, CHOPPED (ABOUT 3/4 CUP)

3/4 CUP BELGIAN OR BELGIAN-STYLE BEER, SUCH AS CHIMAY BLEU, OMMEGANG, OR DUVEL

1/2 CUP REDUCED-SODIUM CHICKEN BROTH

1/4 TEASPOON DRIED THYME

1/4 CUP CRÈME FRAÎCHE

Heat the butter in a large skillet over medium heat. When sizzling, add the apples and sauté until lightly browned, 4 to 5 minutes. Remove and set aside.

Combine the flour, salt, pepper, and nutmeg in a shallow pan (such as a pie plate). Dredge the chicken in the flour mixture, shaking to remove any excess. Heat the canola oil in the same skillet over medium-high heat. Add the chicken in batches; sauté until browned, 3 to 4 minutes per side. Remove. Add the onion; reduce the heat to medium-low. Sauté until lightly browned and softened, 3 to 4 minutes. Stir in the beer, chicken broth, and thyme. Return the chicken to the skillet; reduce the heat to low. Cook, partially covered, for 20 minutes. Turn the chicken and cook, covered, until no longer pink in the thickest portion when cut with a knife, an additional 20 to 25 minutes. Remove the chicken to a platter and cover to keep warm.

Boil the accumulated cooking juices over medium-high heat to reduce slightly, 2 to 3 minutes. Reduce the heat to low; whisk the crème fraîche into the cooking juices and add the apples. Cook for 5 minutes. Pour over the chicken and serve.

MAKE AHEAD Make this recipe through the point of cooking the chicken until no longer pink. Refrigerate the chicken and the sautéed apples separately, covered, then reheat the chicken when ready and proceed as directed.

SERVE WITH The Belgians like to serve everything with fries, but roasted potatoes make an excellent accompaniment. Add a tossed salad with a mustard vinaigrette and crusty bread.

Use Hungarian paprika for this recipe for a truly authentic flavor. The banana pepper mimics those used in Hungary and adds just a hint of heat.

Chicken Paprikash

MAKES 4 SERVINGS

❄

1 TABLESPOON CANOLA OIL

1 TABLESPOON SALTED BUTTER

ONE 3- TO 3¹/₂-POUND CHICKEN, CUT IN PIECES

¹/₂ TEASPOON SALT

¹/₈ TEASPOON FRESHLY GROUND PEPPER

1 LARGE ONION, CHOPPED (ABOUT 1¹/₂ CUPS)

1 BANANA PEPPER, CHOPPED (ABOUT ¹/₄ CUP)

1 LARGE GARLIC CLOVE, CHOPPED (ABOUT 1¹/₂ TEASPOONS)

1¹/₂ TABLESPOONS SWEET HUNGARIAN PAPRIKA

2 LARGE ROMA TOMATOES, DICED (ABOUT 1 CUP)

ONE 14-OUNCE CAN REDUCED-SODIUM CHICKEN BROTH (1³/₄ CUPS)

2 TABLESPOONS ALL-PURPOSE FLOUR

¹/₂ CUP SOUR CREAM

Heat the canola oil and butter in a large skillet over medium heat. When sizzling, sauté the chicken in batches, seasoned with the salt and pepper, until golden brown, 3 to 4 minutes per side. Remove.

Add the onion; reduce the heat to low. Sauté, stirring occasionally, until softened, about 5 minutes. Stir in the banana pepper; sauté for 1 minute. Add the garlic; stir to combine. Sprinkle with the paprika; stir again. Sauté until fragrant, 30 seconds to 1 minute. Stir in the tomatoes.

Return the chicken to the skillet in a single layer; turn to coat both sides of the chicken with the paprika mixture. Add 1¹/₂ cups of the chicken broth; increase the heat briefly to medium until just boiling. Reduce the heat to low; cook, covered, turning once during cooking, until the chicken is no longer pink when cut with a knife in the thickest portion, about 40 minutes.

Remove the chicken to a platter; cover with aluminum foil to keep warm.

Whisk the remaining ¹/₄ cup chicken broth with the flour in a small bowl until smooth and lump free; whisk into the pan juices. Increase the heat to medium-high and boil until thickened, 2 to 3 minutes. Remove from the heat; whisk in the sour cream. Pour over the chicken; serve immediately.

MAKE AHEAD Complete the recipe except for adding the sour cream. Refrigerate, covered, and then reheat until just warmed through. Remove the chicken to a platter; whisk in the sour cream and pour over the chicken.

SERVE WITH Spaetzle or noodles to soak up the paprika-laced sauce. Green beans or peas would go well with this dish.

Attribution of this recipe's name is varied. Some connect it to a British officer who served in India; others claim that the word "captain" comes from the abbreviation cap'n, which, in turn, is derived from capon. Somehow, whatever the source of the name, this British Empire–style interpretation of curry has long been part of the repertoire of classic American recipes.

Country Captain Chicken

MAKES 4 SERVINGS

❋

1/3 CUP ALL-PURPOSE FLOUR

1 TEASPOON DRIED THYME

3/4 TEASPOON SALT

1/4 TEASPOON FRESHLY
GROUND PEPPER

4 BONE-IN, SKIN-ON
CHICKEN THIGHS

2 BONE-IN, SKIN-ON CHICKEN
BREAST HALVES, CUT IN HALF
ACROSS THE BONE IF LARGE

1 TABLESPOON SALTED BUTTER

1 TABLESPOON CANOLA OIL

1 LARGE ONION, CHOPPED
(ABOUT 1 1/2 CUPS)

1/2 GREEN BELL PEPPER,
CHOPPED (ABOUT 3/4 CUP)

2 LARGE GARLIC CLOVES,
CHOPPED (ABOUT
1 TABLESPOON)

2 TEASPOONS MINCED GINGER

1 1/2 TABLESPOONS
CURRY POWDER

1/2 TEASPOON CINNAMON

PINCH CAYENNE

ONE 14 1/2-OUNCE CAN DICED
TOMATOES IN JUICE

1/4 CUP DRIED CURRANTS

Mix the flour, thyme, salt, and pepper together in a shallow dish. Dredge the chicken in the flour mixture on both sides. Heat the butter and canola oil in a large skillet over medium-high heat. Add the chicken in batches; sauté until browned, 3 to 4 minutes per side. Remove. Pour off all but 2 tablespoons of fat. Add the onion and bell pepper; reduce the heat to medium. Sauté until softened, 4 to 5 minutes. Stir in the garlic and ginger; sauté until fragrant, 30 seconds to 1 minute. Add the curry powder, cinnamon, and cayenne; stir to blend. Add the tomatoes; stir to blend. Add the chicken, skin side up; reduce the heat to low and cook, covered, for 30 minutes. Stir in the currants and cook, covered, until the chicken is no longer pink in the thickest portion when cut with a knife, an additional 5 to 10 minutes.

MAKE AHEAD Make the whole recipe ahead and gently reheat to serve. Don't heat it too long or the chicken breasts will dry out. Another option is to use a total of 8 bone-in, skin-on thighs instead of the breast and thigh combination. Since thighs take much longer cooking, the pot can sit and simmer until you're ready to serve.

SERVE WITH Rice to soak up the sauce, and cucumbers dressed with cream or yogurt to complement the curry seasoning.

*C*oconut milk and chicken seem to have a special affinity for each other, with the coconut adding just the right touch of mildly nutty richness, enhanced in this recipe by orange juice, and spiked by both coarsely ground black pepper and cayenne.

Brazilian Chicken

✵

2 TABLESPOONS OLIVE OIL

1 LARGE ONION, CHOPPED
(ABOUT 1¹/₂ CUPS)

1 GREEN BELL PEPPER,
CUT IN ¹/₂-INCH DICE
(ABOUT 1¹/₂ CUPS)

1 LARGE GARLIC CLOVE,
CHOPPED (ABOUT
1¹/₂ TEASPOONS)

6 MEDIUM ROMA TOMATOES,
CUT IN ¹/₂-INCH DICE
(ABOUT 2 CUPS)

6 TO 8 BONELESS, SKINLESS
CHICKEN THIGHS, CUT IN
1¹/₂-INCH CUBES

1 TEASPOON SALT

¹/₂ TEASPOON COARSE, FRESHLY
GROUND PEPPER

GENEROUS PINCH CAYENNE

ONE 5¹/₂-OUNCE CAN
COCONUT MILK (OR ³/₄ CUP)

¹/₂ CUP ORANGE JUICE

1 TABLESPOON CHOPPED
CILANTRO, PLUS 2 TABLESPOONS
CILANTRO LEAVES

Heat the olive oil in a Dutch oven over medium heat. Add the onion and sauté until softened, 4 to 5 minutes. Add the bell pepper; sauté for 1 minute. Add the garlic; sauté until fragrant, 30 seconds to 1 minute. Add the tomatoes; cook until the tomatoes begin to soften and yield their juices, 3 to 4 minutes. Add the chicken, seasoned with the salt, pepper, and cayenne; stir to combine. Stir in the coconut milk and orange juice. Bring just to a boil; reduce the heat to low and cook, covered, for 40 minutes. Stir in the chopped cilantro and cook, covered, for an additional 5 minutes. Garnish with the cilantro leaves and serve.

MAKE AHEAD Make the recipe up to the point of adding the chopped cilantro. Refrigerate, covered; reheat when ready to serve. Add the chopped cilantro and complete as directed.

SERVE WITH Lots of rice to soak up the coconut sauce, and reinforce the tropical feel with an avocado-topped salad.

Jessica Harris, an acclaimed African-American historian and cookbook author, is known for her Chicken Yassa.

This recipe has its origins in Senegal, a West African country with French influences. The Habañero chile, one of the hottest peppers available, gives the chicken a characteristic punch. Vary the amount depending on personal preference.

Chicken Yassa

MAKES 4 SERVINGS

❋

½ CUP LEMON JUICE
(ABOUT 2 LEMONS)

3 TABLESPOONS PEANUT OR
CANOLA OIL

3 LARGE ONIONS, SLICED

1 HABAÑERO CHILE, SLICED,
PLUS 1 TEASPOON CHOPPED
HABAÑERO (SEEDED AND
MEMBRANES REMOVED, IF
DESIRED)

ONE 3½- TO 4-POUND
CHICKEN, CUT IN PIECES

½ TEASPOON SALT

¼ TEASPOON FRESHLY
GROUND PEPPER

⅔ CUP REDUCED-SODIUM
CHICKEN BROTH

3 LARGE CARROTS, PEELED AND
CUT IN ¾-INCH PIECES

Combine the lemon juice, 2 tablespoons of the peanut oil, a handful of the sliced onions, and the sliced habañero in a 1-gallon self-sealing plastic bag to make a marinade. Add the chicken; turn and squeeze to coat. Marinate for 1 hour in the refrigerator, turning occasionally.

Remove the chicken from the marinade and pat dry; reserve the marinade. Season the chicken with the salt and pepper. Heat the remaining 1 tablespoon peanut oil in a Dutch oven over medium-high heat; sauté the chicken in batches until browned, 3 to 4 minutes per side. Remove. Add the remaining sliced onions; sauté until softened, scraping up the browned bits on the bottom with a wooden spoon to prevent scorching, 3 to 4 minutes. Add the chopped habañero to taste. (Use more or less of the chile, depending on your personal preferences for heat level. Including the seeds and membrane makes the dish hotter.)

Strain the marinade into the onions; cook until most of the liquid is evaporated, 3 to 4 minutes. Return the chicken to the pot; add the chicken broth and carrots. Stir to blend. Reduce the heat to low and cook, covered, turning occasionally, until the chicken is no longer pink when cut in the thickest portion with a knife, 35 to 45 minutes. Remove the chicken to a platter and cover to keep warm.

Increase the heat to high; boil until the liquid is reduced by one-third. Return the chicken to the pot and serve.

MAKE AHEAD Marinate the chicken for several hours or complete the recipe and refrigerate, covered, until ready to reheat over low heat.

SERVE WITH Rice and flat bread.

*D*oro wat hails from Ethiopia. When the intricate blend of spices perfumes your kitchen, you'll feel transported to a different world. With one bite, you'll want to stay.

The berbere spice mix is an adaptation of the authentic Ethiopian blend that works well without a spice cupboard's worth of ingredients. I've included a more complex version at the end of the recipe for those who like to putter in the kitchen. The second rendition starts with whole spices, toasts them, and then freshly grinds them for optimum effect.

MAKES 8 SERVINGS

❋

BERBERE SPICE MIX I

4 TEASPOONS PAPRIKA

2¹/₂ TEASPOONS
CURRY POWDER

1 TEASPOON GROUND CUMIN

¹/₂ TEASPOON SALT

¹/₄ TO ¹/₂ TEASPOON CAYENNE

¹/₈ TEASPOON CINNAMON

DORO WAT

8 TABLESPOONS (1 STICK)
UNSALTED BUTTER

2 LARGE ONIONS, CHOPPED
(ABOUT 3 CUPS)

2 LARGE GARLIC CLOVES,
PEELED AND LIGHTLY CRUSHED,
PLUS 2 LARGE GARLIC CLOVES,
MINCED (ABOUT 1 TABLESPOON)

THREE ¹/₄-INCH, QUARTER-SIZED
GINGER SLICES, CRUSHED

¹/₈ TEASPOON FENUGREEK
SEEDS, OPTIONAL

3 CARDAMOM SEEDS

Doro Wat

For berbere spice mix I, combine all the ingredients in a small bowl; set aside.

For the doro wat, melt the butter in a Dutch oven over low heat. Add 2 tablespoons of the onions, the crushed garlic cloves, ginger slices, fenugreek seeds (if desired), cardamom seeds, cloves, and cinnamon. Continue to cook until the onions begin to brown and most of the milk solids from the butter have settled to the bottom, about 15 minutes. Remove from the heat; strain into a small bowl. Discard the solids. Skim off any surface foam.

Meanwhile, squeeze the juice from the lemon half over the chicken.

Clean the Dutch oven and place over medium heat. Add 2 tablespoons of the seasoned clarified butter (*niter kibbeh*) and the remaining chopped onions. Sauté, stirring frequently, until the onions brown, about 10 minutes. Add the minced garlic; sauté until fragrant, 30 seconds to 1 minute. Spoon in the remaining niter kibbeh, taking care to leave behind any accumulated milk solids on the bottom of the bowl. Stir in the berbere spice mixture. Add ¹/₂ cup water; bring to a simmer. Add the chicken and turn to coat. Add the wine; reduce the heat to low. Cook, covered, for 20 minutes; turn the chicken and cook, covered, for an additional 20 minutes. Add the hard-cooked eggs, if desired; turn the chicken and cook until no longer pink in the thickest portion, an additional 10 to 20 minutes. Sprinkle with the pepper and serve.

For berbere spice mixture II, place the cumin seeds, fenugreek seeds, cardamom seeds, coriander seeds, peppercorns, cloves, and allspice berries in a Dutch oven. Heat over medium heat; toast the spices until aromatic, 2 to 3 minutes. Remove from the pan; let cool for several minutes. Place in a small spice grinder or clean coffee grinder; pulse to coarsely grind. Add the chiles and paprika; pulse until the chiles are broken into small pieces. Add the dried minced onion, salt, ginger, turmeric, and cinnamon; pulse until well blended. Measure out 2¹/2 tablespoons to use in the doro wat; reserve the remainder in a tightly sealed container for later use.

MAKE AHEAD Simply refrigerate the entire completed dish, covered, until ready to serve. Reheat gently, over low heat, until heated through, 25 to 30 minutes.

SERVE WITH The unique, spongy bread native to Ethiopia, if you can find it, for dipping in the spicy, buttery sauce. Otherwise, serve a soft Middle Eastern flat bread, such as pita, or an Indian naan. Add a sliced tomato salad and rice.

2 CLOVES

PINCH CINNAMON

1/2 LEMON

3 BONE-IN, SKINLESS CHICKEN
BREAST HALVES

3 BONE-IN, SKINLESS CHICKEN
THIGHS

3 BONE-IN, SKINLESS CHICKEN
DRUMSTICKS

1/2 CUP WHITE WINE

6 HARD-COOKED LARGE EGGS,
OPTIONAL

1/2 TEASPOON COARSE, FRESHLY
GROUND PEPPER

BERBERE SPICE MIX II

1 1/2 TEASPOONS CUMIN SEEDS

3/4 TEASPOON FENUGREEK SEEDS

1/4 TEASPOON CARDAMOM SEEDS

1/4 TEASPOON CORIANDER SEEDS

1/4 TEASPOON BLACK
PEPPERCORNS

3 CLOVES

3 WHOLE ALLSPICE BERRIES

4 TO 6 DRIED RED CHILES

1 1/2 TABLESPOONS SWEET
PAPRIKA, PREFERABLY
HUNGARIAN

1 TABLESPOON DRIED MINCED
ONION

3/4 TEASPOON SALT

1/2 TEASPOON GROUND GINGER

1/4 TEASPOON TURMERIC

1/8 TEASPOON CINNAMON

5 Roasted and Baked Dinners

Older recipes call for stuffing a bird—hence the term "stuffing"—before cooking. From a quality and food-safety standpoint, preparing the chicken and the stuffing in their own individual containers is a much better option. That way, the chicken breast does not overcook while the cook tries to get the stuffing thoroughly heated—something that often happens when these foods are cooked together.

Fundamentally, what follows is a one-roasting-pan recipe for the brined chicken. The stuffing is an added bonus. Make one or make them both as the mood and occasion suit.

Bourbon-Brined Chicken with Cornbread Stuffing

MAKES 6 SERVINGS

※

BOURBON-BRINED CHICKEN

¹/₂ CUP KOSHER SALT, PREFERABLY DIAMOND CRYSTAL

2 TABLESPOONS PACKED LIGHT BROWN SUGAR

1 TEASPOON DRIED THYME

PINCH CAYENNE

¹/₂ CUP PLUS 1 TABLESPOON BOURBON

ONE 4¹/₂- TO 5¹/₂-POUND CHICKEN

1 GRANNY SMITH APPLE

1 MEDIUM ONION

1 TABLESPOON SALTED BUTTER

1 TABLESPOON CORNSTARCH

For the chicken, combine the salt, brown sugar, 3/4 teaspoon of the thyme, and the cayenne in a medium bowl. Stir in 5¹/2 cups water to dissolve the salt; add the ¹/2 cup bourbon. Rinse the inner cavity of the chicken to remove any pooled blood; place the chicken in a 1-gallon self-sealing plastic bag and pour the brine over the chicken. Squeeze the bag to remove all excess air, bringing the brine up and around the chicken to cover the bird; seal the bag securely and place in a large bowl for support. Refrigerate for 5 to 6 hours.

Heat the oven to 375°F.

Core and halve the apple and reserve one half for the stuffing; cut the other half into large wedges. Slice the onion. Remove the chicken from the brine and pat dry. Discard the brine. Insert the apple wedges and several onion slices in the cavity of the chicken; sprinkle the remaining ¹/4 teaspoon thyme in the cavity. Place the remaining onion slices in the bottom of a medium shallow roasting pan. Rub the

4 TABLESPOONS (1/2 STICK)
SALTED BUTTER

1 MEDIUM ONION, CHOPPED
(ABOUT 3/4 CUP)

2 LARGE CELERY STALKS,
CHOPPED (ABOUT 1 CUP)

1/3 CUP CHOPPED PECANS

1 TEASPOON DRIED,
RUBBED SAGE

1/2 TEASPOON POULTRY
SEASONING

1/8 TEASPOON SALT

1/8 TEASPOON FRESHLY
GROUND PEPPER

4 1/2 CUPS PACKAGED
CORNBREAD STUFFING (FROM A
16-OUNCE BAG)

ONE 14-OUNCE CAN REDUCED-
SODIUM CHICKEN BROTH

1/2 CUP APPLE CIDER

chicken with the butter and place it on top of the onion slices. Roast for 1 1/2 to 1 3/4 hours, until a thermometer reaches 180°F when inserted in the thickest portion of the thigh and the juices run clear. Remove the chicken to a platter.

For the stuffing, while the chicken is roasting, melt the butter in a large skillet over medium-low heat. Add the onion and celery; sauté for 4 minutes. Meanwhile, chop the reserved apple half; add to the skillet. Sauté the mixture until the onion and celery are softened, an additional 2 to 3 minutes. Stir in the pecans, sage, poultry seasoning, salt, and pepper. Place the cornbread stuffing in a 1 1/2-quart baking dish; add the sautéed mixture. Toss with 1 cup of the chicken broth and the apple cider. Cover with aluminum foil; bake simultaneously with the chicken for 45 minutes, removing the aluminum foil during the last 15 minutes of baking.

For the gravy, add the remaining chicken broth to the roasting pan. Add 1/2 cup water and the remaining 1 tablespoon bourbon to the pan; bring to a boil over medium-high heat, scraping up any browned bits from the bottom of the pan. Dissolve the cornstarch in 2 tablespoons water and whisk into the pan; continue to cook until thickened, about 1 minute. Strain and serve with the chicken and stuffing.

MAKE AHEAD The chicken can be brined the day before, if desired; drain the brine and refrigerate in the same self-sealing bag until ready to roast. For crisper skin, refrigerate the chicken after brining, uncovered, for 6 to 8 hours.

SERVE WITH Buttered carrots and a tossed salad garnished with dried cranberries to round out the menu.

Across the northern tier of the United States and up into Canada, maple trees are tapped for their sap every spring. When the temperatures are just right, the "sugaring" begins. Once concentrated into an amber syrup, this intensely sweet ingredient is ready to be used by creative cooks in a number of ways that extend well beyond the usual pancake topping. Combined with mustard, butter, and sage, it adds a subtle richness to a basted bird. Try this combination on roasted pork tenderloin as well.

Maple-Basted Roast Chicken

MAKES 4 SERVINGS

✳

2 TABLESPOONS MAPLE SYRUP

1 TABLESPOON DIJON MUSTARD

1 TABLESPOON SALTED BUTTER, MELTED

1 TEASPOON DRIED, RUBBED SAGE

1/4 TEASPOON SALT

1/8 TEASPOON FRESHLY GROUND PEPPER

ONE 3 1/2- TO 4-POUND CHICKEN

1 SMALL ONION, CUT IN HALF

1 CUP REDUCED-SODIUM CHICKEN BROTH

1 TABLESPOON CORNSTARCH

Heat the oven to 375°F.

Stir together the maple syrup, Dijon mustard, melted butter, 1/2 teaspoon of the sage, the salt, and pepper in a small bowl; set aside.

Rinse the chicken cavity to remove any pooled blood; pat dry. Place the chicken on a rack in a medium, shallow roasting pan. Place the onion in the cavity of the chicken along with the remaining 1/2 teaspoon sage. Pour the broth and 1/2 cup water into the roasting pan. Roast for 40 minutes. Baste with the maple mixture; roast for an additional 15 minutes. Baste again; roast for an additional 15 minutes. Baste with the remaining maple mixture; roast for an additional 10 to 20 minutes, or until a thermometer registers 180°F when inserted in the thickest portion of the thigh and the juices run clear. Remove the chicken to a platter. Remove the rack.

Mix 2 tablespoons water with the cornstarch in a small bowl; set aside. Add 1 cup water to the roasting pan. Scrape the bottom to combine the drippings; tilt the pan and skim off some of the surface fat with a spoon. Bring the liquid to a boil over medium heat. Whisk in the cornstarch mixture; cook until thickened, about 1 minute. Serve with the chicken.

MAKE AHEAD Have the chicken all ready in its roaster and the basting mixture mixed and ready to use. Proceed as directed when ready to roast.

SERVE WITH A spiced pecan and goat cheese–topped salad and mashed sweet potatoes.

In this easily put together dish, orange and spice–laden butter bastes a roasting hen, then honey and olives add sweet and salty notes to the glistening bird before serving. While Israel is the official source for this recipe, its ingredients are typical of either side of the Mediterranean basin.

Honey and Orange Roast Chicken

1 ORANGE

1 TABLESPOON SALTED BUTTER, SOFTENED

1 LARGE GARLIC CLOVE, MINCED (ABOUT 1^1/$_2$ TEASPOONS)

^{1}/$_2$ TEASPOON SALT

^{1}/$_2$ TEASPOON CINNAMON

ONE 3^1/$_2$- TO 4-POUND CHICKEN

2 LARGE ONIONS, CUT IN 3/4-INCH WEDGES

1 TABLESPOON HONEY

^{1}/$_2$ CUP PITTED KALAMATA OLIVES

Heat the oven to 375°F. Grate the orange; reserve 1 teaspoon zest. Juice the orange; reserve ^{1}/$_4$ cup juice and the juiced shell.

Combine the orange zest, butter, garlic, ^{1}/$_4$ teaspoon of the salt, and ^{1}/$_4$ teaspoon of the cinnamon in a small bowl. Rinse the chicken to remove any pooled blood and pat dry. Work the orange butter under the skin of the breast, thigh, and upper drumstick portion of the chicken. Place the reserved orange shell in the chicken cavity. Scatter the onion wedges on the bottom of a shallow roasting pan; place the chicken on a rack in the pan. Pour in 1 cup water. Roast the chicken for 1 hour.

Meanwhile, combine the reserved orange juice, the honey, remaining ^{1}/$_4$ teaspoon salt, and remaining ^{1}/$_4$ teaspoon cinnamon in a small saucepan. Heat over low heat until the honey is dissolved, stirring constantly.

After the chicken has roasted for 1 hour, scatter the olives in the bottom of the roasting pan. Baste the chicken with the orange-and-honey mixture; return to the oven for 10 minutes. Remove and pour the remaining orange-and-honey mixture over the chicken. Bake for an additional 10 to 20 minutes, or until a thermometer inserted in the thigh registers 180°F and the juices run clear. Serve with the onions and olives scattered around the chicken and the pan juices on the side.

MAKE AHEAD Have the chicken prepped and on the rack in the roasting pan. Refrigerate, covered, until ready. Roast as directed.

SERVE WITH Israeli couscous and green beans tossed with almonds.

Reading a copy of *Gourmet* magazine on a plane trip to France, I spotted a recipe for quail with figs. Once installed at home in Provence, off I went to the Vaison market, where the vendors offered fresh, ripe figs for sale. I decided immediately to try my hand at chicken with figs for that night's dinner.

Provençal Chicken with Figs

MAKES 4 SERVINGS

※

2 TABLESPOONS OLIVE OIL

2 OUNCES THICK-SLICED BACON, CUT IN 1/4-INCH STRIPS (ABOUT 1/2 CUP)

8 SMALL SHALLOTS (OR 4 LARGE SHALLOTS, HALVED)

2 TABLESPOONS BALSAMIC VINEGAR

3/4 CUP RED WINE

ONE 3 1/2- TO 4-POUND CHICKEN

1/2 TEASPOON SALT

1/4 TEASPOON FRESHLY GROUND PEPPER

8 FRESH FIGS, HALVED

Heat the oven to 375°F.

Heat 1 tablespoon of the olive oil in a flameproof, medium roasting pan over medium heat. Add the bacon and sauté for 2 minutes, stirring frequently. Add the shallots and sauté for an additional 2 minutes. Add the balsamic vinegar and cook for 2 minutes, stirring frequently. Add the wine and bring to a boil. Remove from the heat and add the chicken, seasoned with the salt and pepper. Drizzle with the remaining 1 tablespoon olive oil. Roast for 45 minutes. Add the figs, cut side up, and baste with the cooking juices. Baste again after 15 minutes. Roast until a thermometer registers 180°F when inserted in the thickest portion of the thigh and the juices run clear, an additional 20 to 30 minutes. Remove the chicken, figs, and shallots to a platter and bring the juices to a boil over medium-high heat. Reduce the liquid to about 3/4 cup. Pour over the chicken and serve.

MAKE AHEAD Complete the recipe through bringing the wine to a boil. Cool the mixture; add the chicken to the pan. Refrigerate, covered. When ready, drizzle with the olive oil and roast as directed.

SERVE WITH Potatoes and carrots, cut in chunks, tossed in olive oil, and roasted in the same oven.

The Nyons market in Provence is one of my favorites. While I'm there, I make a detour to the local cooperative and stock up on their fabulous black olives. Because I always over-buy, I invented this recipe to use up the surplus, loving the fact that the chicken effortlessly browns itself in the roasting pan while the wine and tomatoes cook into a delectable stewlike sauce.

The French normally serve their olives unpitted in rustic dishes like this. Back in the States, where Nyons olives can be hard to find, I use pitted Kalamata olives instead.

Nyons Chicken

Heat the oven to 375°F.

Blend the tomato paste, Pernod, herbes de Provence, minced garlic, salt, and pepper together in a small bowl. Stir in the olive oil.

Scatter the garlic cloves on the bottom of a medium, shallow roasting pan; pour in the wine. Arrange the chicken, skin side up, in a single layer in the pan. Brush the chicken with the tomato paste mixture.

Bake for 30 minutes. Remove from the oven and spoon the diced tomatoes and juice around the chicken. Scatter the olives and capers over all. Return to the oven and bake for an additional 20 to 30 minutes, or until the chicken is no longer pink in the thickest portion when cut with a knife.

Serve in a decorative shallow serving bowl or platter, garnished with the chopped parsley and parsley sprigs.

MAKE AHEAD Place the garlic cloves and wine in the roaster; top with the chicken and brush with the tomato paste mixture. Refrigerate, covered, until ready to bake. Proceed with the recipe as directed.

SERVE WITH A crisp salad tossed with extra virgin olive oil and lemon juice, then sprinkled with freshly grated Parmigiano-Reggiano. In our area of Provence, *épeutre*—similar to Italian farro or American spelt—is often served on the side but rice or pasta will soak up the sauce equally well. The local ladder-shaped bread, *fougasse*, is a perfect accompaniment. In America, focaccia—a close cousin—is just as tasty.

2 TABLESPOONS SALT-PACKED
CAPERS, RINSED AND SOAKED
FOR 15 MINUTES

2 TABLESPOONS CHOPPED
FRESH ITALIAN PARSLEY, PLUS
WHOLE SPRIGS

I first had a dish similar to this one at a dinner party in France where the hostess used a locally cured and sliced ham. While I use prosciutto, any high-quality equivalent will do.

Ham-Wrapped Chicken and Endive Gratinée

MAKES 4 SERVINGS

※

1 CUP FRESH BREAD CRUMBS

1 TABLESPOON
SALTED BUTTER, MELTED

2 OUNCES GRUYÈRE OR
EMMENTALER, SHREDDED
(ABOUT ½ CUP)

1 OUNCE PARMIGIANO-
REGGIANO, GRATED
(ABOUT ¼ CUP)

FOUR 6-OUNCE BONELESS,
SKINLESS CHICKEN BREAST
HALVES

¼ TEASPOON SALT

⅛ TEASPOON FRESHLY
GROUND PEPPER

8 THIN SLICES PROSCIUTTO

4 ENDIVE SPEARS, CORED AND
PARBOILED (SEE NOTE)

½ CUP HEAVY CREAM

1 TABLESPOON DIJON MUSTARD

Heat the oven to 375°F. Lightly grease a 12 × 8-inch glass baking dish.

Toss the bread crumbs with the butter until blended in a medium bowl. Stir in the Gruyère and Parmesan; set aside.

Season the chicken breasts with the salt and pepper and wrap each one with a slice of prosciutto. Wrap each endive with a slice of prosciutto and arrange alternately with the chicken breasts in a row in the bottom of the baking dish. Stir the cream and mustard together in a small bowl; pour over the endive and chicken. Cover with aluminum foil and bake for 40 to 45 minutes, or until the chicken is no longer pink in the thickest portion when cut with a knife. Remove from the oven; uncover.

Heat the broiler. Sprinkle the endive and chicken with the bread-crumb-and-cheese mixture. Broil 8 to 10 inches from the broiler element until well browned and crisp, 3 to 5 minutes.

MAKE AHEAD Pour the cream and mustard over the chicken and endive in the baking dish and refrigerate, covered, until ready to bake. When ready, bake as directed, allowing 5 to 10 minutes extra cooking time.

SERVE WITH Rice and a salad tossed with apples and walnuts.

NOTE To parboil the endive, fill a medium saucepan half full of water and bring to a boil over medium-high heat. Add 2 tablespoons lemon juice and the endive spears. Reduce the heat to medium and gently boil for 10 minutes. Drain and let cool slightly.

This recipe starts out with a definite Scandinavian bent, full of cream, mustard, and dried dill, but takes on a sunnier, Mediterranean character with the addition of artichokes and capers. Where it fits in a global perspective is a bit of a mystery, but there's no question as to its appeal.

Chicken Breasts and Artichokes with Dill and Capers

MAKES 4 SERVINGS

✳

FOUR 6-OUNCE BONELESS,
SKINLESS CHICKEN BREAST
HALVES

$^1/_4$ TEASPOON SALT

$^1/_8$ TEASPOON FRESHLY
GROUND PEPPER

ONE 9-OUNCE PACKAGE FROZEN
ARTICHOKE HEARTS, THAWED

$^1/_4$ CUP HEAVY CREAM

2 TEASPOONS LEMON JUICE

2 TABLESPOONS
DIJON MUSTARD

1 TABLESPOON DRIED
DILL WEED

$^1/_2$ CUP WHITE WINE

3 TABLESPOONS CAPERS,
PREFERABLY SALT-PACKED,
RINSED

Heat the oven to 350°F. Season the chicken with the salt and pepper; arrange in a single layer in the bottom of a 12 × 8-inch glass or ceramic baking pan. Scatter the artichokes around the chicken.

Stir the cream and lemon juice together in a medium bowl; let rest until thickened, 1 to 2 minutes. Stir in the mustard and dried dill until well blended. Whisk in the white wine and add the capers. Pour the dill mixture over the chicken. Bake for 40 to 50 minutes, or until the chicken is no longer pink in the thickest portion when cut with a knife.

MAKE AHEAD Prepare the recipe up to the point of baking and refrigerate, covered, for up to 4 hours, until ready to proceed. Bake as directed.

SERVE WITH Rice, a cucumber salad, and Swedish rye bread.

*P*anko bread crumbs—from Japan—are the secret ingredient for success in this Italian recipe, forming an extra-crisp coating right in the oven. They eliminate the normal step of frying the breaded chicken before baking. Instead, the pounded breasts are prebaked in their cloak of panko crumbs. I've also streamlined the recipe by using bottled marinara sauce. Cutting corners with quality premade products gives an overscheduled cook the gift of extra time.

Chicken Parmigiano

MAKES 4 SERVINGS

✳

2 TABLESPOONS OLIVE OIL

3/4 CUP PANKO BREAD CRUMBS

3/4 CUP FRESHLY GRATED
PARMIGIANO-REGGIANO

1 TEASPOON ITALIAN
SEASONING

1/4 TEASPOON SALT

1/8 TEASPOON FRESHLY
GROUND PEPPER

1 LARGE EGG

2 TABLESPOONS MILK

FOUR 5- TO 6-OUNCE
BONELESS, SKINLESS CHICKEN
BREAST HALVES

1 1/2 CUPS BOTTLED
MARINARA SAUCE

1/4 CUP CHOPPED FRESH BASIL

1 CUP SHREDDED MOZZARELLA

Heat the oven to 400°F. Lightly oil the bottom of a 13 × 9-inch glass baking dish with 1/2 tablespoon of the olive oil.

Mix the panko crumbs, 1/4 cup of the Parmesan, the Italian seasoning, salt, and pepper in a pie pan. Toss with the remaining 1 1/2 tablespoons olive oil until blended. In a separate shallow dish, whisk together the egg and milk. Cut the chicken breast halves in half; pound each piece between two sheets of plastic wrap to a scant 1/2-inch thickness.

Dip the pieces first in the egg mixture and then in the crumb mixture, turning to coat. Arrange in a single layer in the oiled baking dish. Bake for 15 minutes.

Remove from the oven; reduce the heat to 350°F. Spoon the marinara sauce over the breast pieces. Top with the basil, mozzarella, and remaining 1/2 cup Parmesan. Cover with aluminum foil and bake for an additional 10 minutes.

MAKE AHEAD Bread the breasts and arrange in a baking dish. Refrigerate, covered, for up to 5 to 6 hours, then proceed with the recipe as indicated.

SERVE WITH Green beans tossed with olive oil and thyme, a salad, and crusty bread.

*R*olling chicken breasts around a sausage filling is a brilliant maneuver, adding an abundance of flavor and basting the breasts internally for succulently moist meat. Baking the rolls with the pomodoro (tomato) sauce blends all the different elements together.

Tuscan Chicken Rolls with Pomodoro Sauce

MAKES 4 SERVINGS

❈

FOUR 6-OUNCE BONELESS, SKINLESS CHICKEN BREAST HALVES

1/2 POUND MILD OR HOT BULK ITALIAN SAUSAGE

1/4 CUP PINE NUTS

12 FRESH BASIL LEAVES

2 TABLESPOONS OLIVE OIL

1 MEDIUM ONION, CHOPPED (ABOUT 3/4 CUP)

2 LARGE GARLIC CLOVES, CHOPPED (ABOUT 1 TABLESPOON)

1/2 CUP REDUCED-SODIUM CHICKEN BROTH

1/2 CUP WHITE WINE

2 MEDIUM TOMATOES (ABOUT 1/2 POUND), DICED (ABOUT 1 CUP)

3/4 TEASPOON CHOPPED FRESH ROSEMARY (OR 1/4 TEASPOON DRIED ROSEMARY)

3/4 TEASPOON CHOPPED FRESH SAGE (OR 1/4 TEASPOON DRIED SAGE)

1/2 TEASPOON SALT

1/4 TEASPOON FRESHLY GROUND PEPPER

Heat the oven to 400°F.

Flatten each chicken breast, using a rolling pin or meat mallet, between sheets of plastic wrap, until slightly over 1/4 inch thick. Divide the Italian sausage into 4 portions. Flatten each portion and place 1 portion on top of each breast, continuing to flatten and spread the sausage to within 1/2 inch of the edges. Sprinkle each with 1 tablespoon pine nuts; top with 3 basil leaves in a single layer. Roll each up and fasten with toothpicks or kitchen string.

Heat 1 tablespoon of the olive oil in a shallow nonreactive metal baking dish (or a large ovenproof skillet) over medium heat. Add the onion; sauté until tender, 4 to 5 minutes. Add the garlic; sauté until fragrant, 30 seconds to 1 minute. Add the chicken broth and white wine; increase the heat to high and reduce by half, 3 to 5 minutes. Add the tomatoes and cook for an additional 1 minute. Remove the sauce from the heat and stir in the rosemary, sage, 1/4 teaspoon of the salt, and 1/8 teaspoon of the pepper.

Arrange the breasts, sealed side down, in the pan with the sauce. Sprinkle the breasts with the remaining 1/4 teaspoon salt and 1/8 teaspoon pepper. Drizzle with the remaining 1 tablespoon olive oil. Bake until the chicken and sausage are no longer pink in the center when cut with a knife, 35 to 40 minutes. Remove the breasts and cover with aluminum foil to keep warm. Place the pan over medium-high heat; boil the tomato sauce to reduce by one-third and thicken slightly, 3 to 4 minutes. Return the breasts to the pan; spoon some of the sauce over the breasts and serve.

MAKE AHEAD Assemble the rolls with the stuffing and prepare the sauce. Let the sauce cool, then arrange the breasts on the sauce and refrigerate, covered, until ready to bake. Proceed as directed, adding about 5 minutes to the baking time.

SERVE WITH Tender baby carrots and focaccia or Tuscan-style bread. Add an olive, mixed greens, and arugula salad dressed with balsamic vinaigrette.

*T*he Italian duo of artichokes and potatoes is even better when combined with chicken. Enhanced by capers, garlic, and rosemary and braised with a bit of white wine, this meal-in-a-pan is hard to beat.

I've called for salt-packed capers because their larger size works well in this recipe and their flavor is truer than those packed in brine. They need to be soaked briefly to remove the excess salt. If you can't find them, feel free to use the ones in liquid. Make sure to rinse the brined capers thoroughly, but soaking is not necessary.

Italian-Baked Chicken

MAKES 4 SERVINGS

⁂

4 TEASPOONS SALT-PACKED
CAPERS

6 TO 8 SMALL RED BOILING
POTATOES (ABOUT 1 POUND),
QUARTERED

ONE 9-OUNCE PACKAGE FROZEN
ARTICHOKE HEARTS, THAWED

3 LARGE GARLIC CLOVES,
CHOPPED (ABOUT
1$^{1}/_{2}$ TABLESPOONS)

2 TEASPOONS CHOPPED FRESH
ROSEMARY (OR $^{3}/_{4}$ TEASPOON
DRIED ROSEMARY)

$^{1}/_{2}$ TEASPOON SALT

$^{1}/_{4}$ TEASPOON FRESHLY
GROUND PEPPER

2 TABLESPOONS OLIVE OIL

1 TABLESPOON LEMON JUICE

4 BONE-IN, SKIN-ON
CHICKEN THIGHS

2 BONE-IN, SKIN-ON CHICKEN
BREAST HALVES

$^{1}/_{2}$ CUP WHITE WINE

Heat the oven to 375°F. Cover the capers with water in a small dish and soak for 15 minutes. Drain.

Scatter the potatoes and artichokes over the bottom of a flameproof roasting pan. Chop the garlic and rosemary together; divide in half. Sprinkle half of the garlic mixture over the potatoes and artichokes. Sprinkle with the salt and $^{1}/_{8}$ teaspoon of the pepper; toss to coat. Drizzle with 1 tablespoon of the olive oil and the lemon juice; toss again.

Top with the chicken, skin side up, in a single layer. Chop the remaining garlic mixture with the capers and sprinkle over the chicken; rub into the skin. Sprinkle with the remaining $^{1}/_{8}$ teaspoon pepper and drizzle with the remaining 1 tablespoon oil. Pour in the wine along the side of the pan.

Bake for 45 to 55 minutes, or until the chicken is no longer pink in the thickest portion when cut with a knife. Remove the chicken, potatoes, and artichokes to a platter and place the roaster over medium-high heat. Boil the cooking juices until reduced by half, 3 to 4 minutes. Pour over the chicken and serve.

MAKE AHEAD Prepare the recipe up to the point of baking and refrigerate, covered, in the roasting pan up to several hours earlier in the day. Bake when ready.

SERVE WITH Sliced tomatoes and crusty bread.

edolent with the aroma of plump mushrooms, intensely concentrated sun-dried tomatoes, moist morsels of chicken, and topped with golden polenta, this Italian-inspired dish incorporates all the necessary main-course components to be baked and served in a single container, the American deep-dish pie pan.

It is possible to be an absolute one-pot purist and use an ovenproof skillet as the sole cooking container in this recipe, but this would involve reserving ingredients in plates and bowls between cooking steps before assembling everything back together at the end. It's actually simpler to cheat a tiny bit and transfer from skillet to pie pan in a straightforward sequence, as I've done here.

Chicken and Mushroom Polenta Pie

MAKES 4 TO 6 SERVINGS

✳

3 TABLESPOONS OLIVE OIL

TWO 6- TO 8-OUNCE BONELESS, SKINLESS CHICKEN BREAST HALVES, CUT IN 1-INCH CUBES

3/4 TEASPOON ITALIAN SEASONING

3/4 TEASPOON SALT

1/8 TEASPOON FRESHLY GROUND PEPPER

2 LARGE GARLIC CLOVES, MINCED (ABOUT 1 TABLESPOON)

8 OUNCES BABY PORTOBELLO (CREMINI) MUSHROOMS, QUARTERED

1/4 CUP RED WINE

1/2 CUP MARINATED ARTICHOKE HEARTS, CUT IN 3/4-INCH PIECES, WELL DRAINED

1/4 CUP COARSELY CHOPPED SUN-DRIED TOMATOES PACKED IN OIL, WELL DRAINED

1/4 CUP COARSELY CHOPPED PITTED KALAMATA OLIVES

Heat the oven to 350°F.

Heat 2 tablespoons of the olive oil in a large skillet over medium heat. Add the chicken, seasoned with the Italian seasoning, 1/4 teaspoon of the salt, and the pepper. Sauté, turning the chicken occasionally, until golden brown on all sides and cooked through, 6 to 8 minutes. Remove to a deep-dish pie pan.

Add the remaining 1 tablespoon olive oil to the skillet. When hot, add the garlic and sauté until fragrant, 30 seconds to 1 minute. Add the mushrooms; toss to coat with the garlic. Reduce the heat to medium-low; sauté until the mushrooms are beginning to soften, 2 to 3 minutes. Add the red wine, continuing to cook until the mushrooms are softened and all the liquid has evaporated, 6 to 8 minutes. Remove to the pie pan. Top with the artichoke hearts, sun-dried tomatoes, and olives; sprinkle with half the mozzarella.

Add 3 cups water to the skillet; increase the heat to medium-high. Bring to a boil; stir in the remaining $^1/_2$ teaspoon salt. Stir in the cornmeal; continue to cook until well thickened, 5 to 8 minutes. Remove from the heat; stir in the milk and spoon into the pie pan. Cover with aluminum foil and bake for 20 minutes. Remove the foil; sprinkle with the remaining mozzarella. Bake for an additional 10 minutes, until the cheese is melted and the pie is piping hot. Bring to the table; cut in wedges and serve, spooning any filling remaining in the pie plate over the polenta.

MAKE AHEAD Refrigerate the foil-topped pie, unbaked. About 50 minutes before serving, preheat the oven. Bake for 30 minutes, covered with the foil; remove the foil and top with the remaining cheese. Bake for an additional 10 minutes, until the cheese is melted and the pie is piping hot.

SERVE WITH A salad tossed with a balsamic vinaigrette and crusty bread. When entertaining, wrap melon in prosciutto for a quick hors d'oeuvre and pour a glass of Prosecco. Serve your favorite red wine with the pie.

1 CUP SHREDDED MOZZARELLA

3/4 CUP STONE-GROUND CORNMEAL

1/3 CUP MILK

*H*ere is a lovely dish, both in looks and taste. Red tomatoes, pale green fennel, and yellow quince form the base for browned chicken flecked with garlic and pepper.

Two ingredients mark this recipe as Mediterranean; the second places it closer to Greece or Turkey. The first is quince, a golden fruit used primarily for jellies and pastes such as Membrillo from Spain, but excellent baked with savory ingredients like chicken. Since quince is found only in later fall, tart apples, which the fruit resembles, can be substituted at other times of year. The second ingredient is Aleppo—sometimes called halaby—pepper, sold as crushed dried flakes with a flavor a bit zingier than ancho chiles.

Baked Chicken with Fennel and Quince

MAKES 4 SERVINGS

✳

2 LARGE GARLIC CLOVES, CHOPPED (ABOUT 1 TABLESPOON)

1¹/₂ TEASPOONS CRUSHED DRIED ALEPPO PEPPER

³/₄ TEASPOON SALT

1 LARGE ONION, CUT IN HALF, THEN IN 1-INCH WEDGES

1 MEDIUM FENNEL BULB, TRIMMED AND CUT IN 1¹/₂-INCH CHUNKS, PLUS 2 TABLESPOONS CHOPPED FENNEL FRONDS

1 QUINCE (OR TART APPLE), CORED AND CUT IN 1-INCH WEDGES

ONE 14¹/₂-OUNCE CAN DICED TOMATOES IN JUICE

¹/₄ CUP SWEET VERMOUTH

ONE 3¹/₂- TO 4-POUND CHICKEN, CUT IN PIECES

1 TABLESPOON OLIVE OIL

Heat the oven to 375°F. Mix together the garlic, Aleppo pepper, and salt in a small bowl.

Scatter the onion, fennel chunks, and quince over the bottom of a 13 × 9-inch baking pan; toss with half the garlic mixture. Add the tomatoes with their juice and the sweet vermouth; stir to blend. Top with the chicken, skin side up. Sprinkle the remaining garlic mixture over the chicken; rub over the skin. Drizzle the chicken with the olive oil. Bake for 50 to 60 minutes, basting occasionally, or until the chicken is no longer pink in the thickest portion when cut with a knife. Garnish with the fennel fronds.

MAKE AHEAD Have everything assembled and ready to put in the oven. Refrigerate, covered. Proceed when ready.

SERVE WITH A torn spinach salad topped with pine nuts and raisins along with rice or orzo.

This is inspired by a traditional Greek dish made with shrimp and feta. Shaped like grains of rice, orzo is really a pasta, perfectly satisfying when paired with tomatoes and oregano. Nestled under feta-topped chicken breasts, it cooks while the chicken bakes, basted by savory cooking juices in the process.

Feta-Topped Chicken with Orzo

MAKES 4 SERVINGS

✳

ONE 14¹/₂-OUNCE CAN DICED
TOMATOES IN JUICE

¹/₂ CUP CHOPPED
GREEN ONIONS

1 LARGE GARLIC CLOVE, MINCED
(ABOUT 1¹/₂ TEASPOONS)

1 TEASPOON DRIED OREGANO

PINCH CINNAMON

PINCH CAYENNE

1 CUP REDUCED-SODIUM
CHICKEN BROTH

1 CUP ORZO

FOUR 10- TO 12-OUNCE
BONE-IN, SKIN-ON CHICKEN
BREAST HALVES

1 TABLESPOON OLIVE OIL

¹/₄ TEASPOON SALT

¹/₈ TEASPOON COARSE, FRESHLY
GROUND PEPPER

4 OUNCES FETA, CRUMBLED
(ABOUT 1 CUP)

Heat the oven to 400°F. Spray a 12 × 8-inch baking dish with nonstick spray.

Stir the tomatoes and their juice, the green onions, garlic, oregano, cinnamon, and cayenne together in a medium bowl; stir in the chicken broth. Spread the orzo over the bottom of the prepared pan; pour the tomato mixture over the orzo. Stir to combine. Top with the chicken, skin side up. Drizzle the chicken with the olive oil; season with the salt and pepper. Bake for 30 minutes. Sprinkle the feta over the top of the chicken; bake for an additional 15 to 20 minutes, or until the chicken is no longer pink in the thickest portion when cut with a knife. Serve.

MAKE AHEAD Although this dish is already quick to prepare, you can speed the process even further by combining the tomatoes, green onions, garlic, oregano, cinnamon, cayenne, and chicken broth in a medium bowl earlier in the day; refrigerate, covered, until ready to bake. Proceed with the recipe as directed.

SERVE WITH Tzatziki—a Greek cucumber salad—and pita bread.

While it is decadently delicious in its own right, I've taken a traditional Greek chicken, custard, and phyllo recipe and added a layer of spinach filling. Now the silky, egg-enriched poultry nestles on a bed of green, adding both eye appeal and extra taste to the completed dish.

In the same way that many dinner-in-a-dish casseroles require a bit of precooking before assembly, the green onions get sautéed before being combined with the spinach, and the butter, flour, and chicken broth cook together in the same skillet to form a foundation for the custard. Ultimately, everything comes together for baking and serving to make a complete main course in one baking dish.

Kotopita

MAKES 8 TO 10 SERVINGS

✳

1 TABLESPOON PLUS ¼ CUP OLIVE OIL

10 TO 12 GREEN ONIONS, WHITE AND TENDER GREEN PORTIONS, CHOPPED (ABOUT 1 CUP)

1 TEASPOON GRATED LEMON ZEST

ONE 16-OUNCE PACKAGE FROZEN CHOPPED SPINACH, THAWED AND SQUEEZED TO REMOVE ALL EXCESS MOISTURE

8 OUNCES FETA, CRUMBLED (ABOUT 2 CUPS)

½ CUP CHOPPED FRESH DILL WEED (OR 3 TABLESPOONS DRIED DILL WEED)

1 TEASPOON SALT

8 TABLESPOONS (1 STICK) SALTED BUTTER, MELTED

¼ CUP ALL-PURPOSE FLOUR

2½ CUPS REDUCED-SODIUM CHICKEN BROTH

Heat the oven to 375°F.

Heat the 1 tablespoon olive oil in a large skillet over medium heat. Add the green onions; sauté until softened, 4 to 5 minutes. Stir in the lemon zest. Remove from the heat and stir in the spinach. Add half of the feta, the dill, and salt; stir to combine. Remove to a bowl.

In the same skillet, add 4 tablespoons of the melted butter. Whisk in the flour; cook over medium-low heat, stirring often, for 2 minutes. Slowly whisk in the broth; increase the heat to medium-high and bring to a boil. Boil, stirring occasionally, for 4 minutes. Pour into a medium bowl; stir in the chicken, the remaining feta, the lemon juice, and nutmeg. Stir in the eggs and set aside.

Combine the remaining 4 tablespoons butter with the remaining ¼ cup olive oil in a small bowl. Brush the bottom and sides of a 13 × 9-inch baking dish with some of the butter mixture. Lay 1 sheet of phyllo in the bottom of the pan; brush with the butter mixture. Lay another sheet on top; brush with the butter mixture. Repeat 8 times, using a total of 10 sheets of phyllo. Spread the spinach mixture over the phyllo; pour the chicken mixture on top of the spinach. Lay 1 sheet of the remaining phyllo on top of the chicken mixture; brush with the butter mixture. Repeat the process with the remaining 9 sheets of phyllo. Drizzle any remaining butter mixture over the top. Bake for 50 to 60 minutes, until the top is golden brown and the chicken layer has set into a custard.

MAKE AHEAD Make the entire dish in advance and refrigerate, covered. Reheat in a 375°F oven, uncovered, until heated through, 20 to 30 minutes. (Tent lightly with aluminum foil if browning too much.)

SERVE WITH Sliced tomatoes and cucumbers sprinkled with freshly chopped mint plus pita bread.

3 CUPS COOKED, CHOPPED CHICKEN

1 TABLESPOON LEMON JUICE

1/2 TEASPOON NUTMEG, PREFERABLY FRESHLY GRATED

3 LARGE EGGS, LIGHTLY BEATEN

TWENTY 14 × 9-INCH SHEETS PHYLLO

Once, while we were traveling with a group in Egypt, the day grew long and our stomachs grew empty. We stopped for an impromptu meal of grilled pigeon, seasoned with a panoply of North African spices. We ate al fresco, watching one of the staff make and bake pita bread in an outdoor wood oven. The meal was fantastic, enhanced no doubt by the fact that we were famished, but memorable under any conditions.

I've changed a few things around in this version, starting with chicken instead of pigeon and roasting it rather than grilling. Using a roasting pan makes adding vegetables, in this case green bell peppers, as easy as can be—something any cook can appreciate.

Egyptian Chicken

MAKES 4 SERVINGS

⁂

ONE 3¹/₂- TO 4-POUND
CHICKEN, QUARTERED

1 LARGE ONION, SLICED

3 LARGE GARLIC CLOVES,
CHOPPED (ABOUT
1¹/₂ TABLESPOONS)

1 TABLESPOON TOMATO PASTE

1 TABLESPOON LEMON JUICE

1¹/₂ TABLESPOONS
GROUND CUMIN

¹/₂ TABLESPOON
GROUND CORIANDER

¹/₂ TEASPOON CAYENNE

¹/₂ TEASPOON SALT

¹/₈ TEASPOON GROUND NUTMEG

¹/₃ CUP OLIVE OIL

2 GREEN BELL PEPPERS,
CUT IN 2-INCH PIECES

Place the chicken and onion in a 1-gallon self-sealing plastic bag. Stir the garlic, tomato paste, and lemon juice together in a small bowl until well blended. Stir in the cumin, coriander, cayenne, salt, and nutmeg. Slowly stir in the olive oil. Pour the mixture into the bag and seal. Squeeze and turn the bag to coat the chicken and onion. Let marinate in the refrigerator for 1 to 4 hours.

Heat the oven to 400°F.

Turn the chicken, onion, and marinade out into a shallow roasting pan; arrange the chicken, skin side up, in a single layer. Roast for 20 minutes. Baste with the cooking juices and scatter the bell peppers around the chicken. Roast for an additional 25 to 35 minutes, until the chicken is no longer pink in the thickest portion when cut with a knife. Remove the chicken, peppers, and onion to a platter and skim off any excess fat. Pour the roasting juices over all and serve.

MAKE AHEAD Time marinating the chicken so that it can go into the oven for baking about 45 minutes before serving. Have the bell peppers cut and ready to add to the roasting pan.

SERVE WITH Couscous and pita bread.

Ground sumac is the star in this Arab recipe from the eastern Mediterranean. Made from sumac berries, it adds a pleasantly puckering acidity and rust-colored hue when rubbed over the chicken before cooking.

Another unique feature is the technique of brushing pita halves with the roasting juices. By briefly baking the bread along with the chicken, the tops of the pita sections crisp while the bottoms take on a hint of the sumac's tartness.

※

2 TABLESPOONS GROUND SUMAC

$^1/_2$ TEASPOON SUGAR

$^1/_2$ TEASPOON SALT

$^1/_4$ TEASPOON GROUND
ALLSPICE

$^1/_4$ TEASPOON CINNAMON

$^1/_4$ TEASPOON GROUND NUTMEG

$^1/_4$ TEASPOON FRESHLY
GROUND PEPPER

ONE $3^1/_2$- TO 4-POUND
CHICKEN, QUARTERED

2 TABLESPOONS OLIVE OIL

2 MEDIUM RED ONIONS, SLICED

2 PITA ROUNDS, CUT IN HALF

$^1/_4$ CUP PINE NUTS

Musakhan

Heat the oven to 400°F. Stir together the sumac, sugar, salt, allspice, cinnamon, nutmeg, and pepper in a small bowl. Sprinkle the chicken with 2 teaspoons of the mixture and rub to spread. Reserve the remainder.

Heat the olive oil in a large ovenproof skillet over medium-low heat. Add the onions and sauté for 5 minutes. Stir in the reserved sumac mixture; cook, stirring often, until the onions are softened, about 15 minutes. Arrange the chicken pieces in a single layer, skin side up, over the onions. Bake for 35 to 40 minutes, or until the chicken is no longer pink in the thickest portion when cut with a knife. Brush the pita halves on one side with some of the cooking juices; arrange around the sides of the skillet. Scatter the pine nuts over the chicken; bake for an additional 5 minutes to warm and crisp the tops of the pitas.

MAKE AHEAD   Prepare the sumac mixture and rub over the chicken as directed. Sauté the onions with the remaining sumac mixture and then let cool. Layer the chicken on top of the onions and refrigerate, covered, until ready to bake. Bake as directed, allowing an extra 5 to 10 minutes cooking time.

SERVE WITH   Sweet potatoes that are baked in the same oven with the chicken. Add a tossed salad sprinkled with sesame seeds.

Jamaica is famous for its grilled chicken and meats, rubbed with a wonderful combination of spices that includes thyme and allspice—sometimes called Jamaican pepper—plus a shot of heat from Scotch bonnet chiles. I've substituted the easily found bottled hot sauce for the Scotch bonnets, and turned this dish into a wonderful one-roasting-pan meal made in the oven. You'll love the subtle way the onion, pineapple, and sweet potatoes pick up and complement the jerk seasoning.

Spicy Roast Jerk Chicken

MAKES 6 SERVINGS

✳

JERK SEASONING

1 TABLESPOON DRIED THYME

1¹/₂ TEASPOONS GROUND ALLSPICE

1¹/₂ TEASPOONS PACKED LIGHT BROWN SUGAR

1 TEASPOON SWEET PAPRIKA

¹/₂ TEASPOON GROUND GINGER

¹/₂ TEASPOON SALT

1 TABLESPOON CIDER VINEGAR

2 TO 3 TEASPOONS HOT SAUCE

1¹/₂ TEASPOONS CANOLA OIL

1 LARGE GARLIC CLOVE, MINCED (ABOUT 1¹/₂ TEASPOONS)

ONE 4¹/₂- TO 5-POUND CHICKEN

1 LARGE RED ONION, CUT IN 1-INCH WEDGES

ONE 20-OUNCE CAN PINEAPPLE CHUNKS IN JUICE, DRAINED AND JUICE RESERVED

3 MEDIUM SWEET POTATOES (ABOUT 1¹/₂ POUNDS)

Heat the oven to 375°F.

For the jerk seasoning, combine the thyme, allspice, brown sugar, paprika, ginger, and salt in a small glass bowl; mix well. Stir in the cider vinegar, hot sauce, canola oil, and garlic.

Rinse the chicken cavity to remove any pooled blood; pat dry. Scatter the onion wedges over the bottom of a large, shallow roasting pan; top with the pineapple chunks. Rub the entire outer surface of the chicken with the jerk seasoning; place the chicken in the roaster. Pour ¹/₄ cup of the reserved pineapple juice in a medium bowl; refrigerate the remainder for another use. Peel the sweet potatoes and cut in 2-inch chunks. Add to the bowl; toss with the juice to thoroughly coat and prevent discoloring. Arrange the sweet potatoes around the chicken in the roaster; discard any remaining juice in the bowl.

Roast, basting the chicken and sweet potatoes occasionally with the accumulated pan juices, for 1¹/₂ hours to 1 hour 40 minutes, or until a thermometer registers 180°F when inserted in the thickest portion of the thigh and the juices run clear. Remove the chicken to a platter, if desired; surround with the onion, pineapple, and sweet potatoes. Tilt the pan and spoon off any surface fat from the pan juices. Spoon some of the pan juices over the onion, pineapple, and sweet potatoes; serve the remaining juices in a pitcher on the side. Carve and serve.

MAKE AHEAD Assemble the recipe, rubbing the chicken with the jerk seasoning and placing it in the roaster with the onion, pineapple, and sweet potatoes. Refrigerate, loosely covered, until ready to roast. Proceed as directed.

SERVE WITH An avocado and hearts of palm salad and corn muffins.

In America, the pumpkin that Jamaicans would typically use can be hard to find fresh and not canned. Butternut squash makes an easily accessible substitute and mellows some of the zing from the fresh-ginger-and-serrano combination.

Jamaican Gingered Chicken

MAKES 4 SERVINGS

※

2 TABLESPOONS MINCED
FRESH GINGER

1 SERRANO CHILE, CHOPPED

2 LARGE GARLIC CLOVES,
CHOPPED (ABOUT
1 TABLESPOON)

1 TABLESPOON LIME JUICE

$1/2$ TEASPOON SALT

1 TEASPOON GROUND GINGER

$1/4$ TEASPOON
GROUND ALLSPICE

$1/2$ MEDIUM BUTTERNUT
SQUASH, PEELED AND CUT IN
$1^1/2$-INCH CHUNKS

1 RED BELL PEPPER,
CUT IN $1^1/2$-INCH CHUNKS
(ABOUT $1^1/2$ CUPS)

1 RED ONION, CUT IN
QUARTERS, THEN IN
1-INCH WEDGES

4 BONE-IN, SKIN-ON
CHICKEN THIGHS

2 BONE-IN, SKIN-ON
CHICKEN BREAST HALVES

1 TABLESPOON OLIVE OIL

Heat the oven to 375°F. Combine the minced fresh ginger, serrano chile, garlic, lime juice, salt, ground ginger, and allspice in a small bowl.

Scatter the squash, bell pepper, and onion over the bottom of a medium roaster. Sprinkle with 1 tablespoon of the ginger mixture; toss to blend. Top with the chicken in a single layer, skin side up. Spoon the remaining ginger mixture evenly over the chicken; spread over the skin. Drizzle with the olive oil. Bake, basting occasionally with any accumulated juices, for 50 to 60 minutes, until the chicken is no longer pink when cut in the thickest portion with a knife.

MAKE AHEAD Assemble the recipe as indicated in the baking dish up to the point of baking. Refrigerate, covered, then drizzle with the olive oil and bake as directed.

SERVE WITH Rice for a great balance to the ginger-and-serrano seasoning plus a green salad.

dding cream to the enchilada sauce qualifies this dish as *suiza*, or Swiss-style, according to Mexican custom. Borrowing from the French, I've turned to crème fraîche as the *suiza* portion of the recipe because it doesn't curdle when thoroughly heated.

In another departure from tradition, I've skipped frying the tortillas before filling. Simply spraying them with nonstick spray keeps them pliable and eliminates a whole preparation step. Folding the tortillas in half instead of rolling them is a common restaurant shortcut and works particularly well when the tortillas are not fried.

Chicken Enchiladas Suizas

MAKES 6 SERVINGS

✳

ONE 16-OUNCE JAR
SALSA VERDE

½ CUP CRÈME FRAÎCHE

3 CUPS COOKED,
DICED CHICKEN

¼ CUP CHOPPED
GREEN ONIONS

12 CORN TORTILLAS

ONE 8-OUNCE PACKAGE
SHREDDED MONTEREY JACK

Heat the oven to 350°F. Spray a 13 × 9-inch baking dish with nonstick spray.

Whisk the salsa verde and ¼ cup of the crème fraîche together in a medium, microwave-safe bowl until well blended to make a sauce. Stir the chicken with ⅓ cup of the sauce, the remaining ¼ cup crème fraîche, and the green onions in a medium bowl until coated. Spray the tortillas on both sides with nonstick spray.

To assemble, lay one tortilla in the prepared baking dish; spoon ¼ cup of the chicken mixture down the center and fold in half to form a half-moon. Repeat with the remaining tortillas, overlapping them slightly in the pan. Cover with aluminum foil and bake for 10 minutes.

Meanwhile, heat the remaining sauce in the microwave until hot, about 2 minutes. Pour the sauce over the enchiladas and top with the cheese. Bake, uncovered, for 10 minutes, or until the cheese is melted and the enchiladas are piping hot.

MAKE AHEAD Assemble as directed. Refrigerate, covered, until ready to bake. Bake, covered, for 15 minutes, then top with the sauce and cheese and bake, uncovered, for 10 minutes.

SERVE WITH Refried beans and a jicama and sliced red onion–topped salad.

Here, the pot is a baking dish, made of glass or ceramic and filled with poblano chiles stuffed with a colorful and salty-sweet filling. Great for family or friends, this dish delivers tons of flavor to the table all in one container.

For better flavor and texture, I've sautéed the filling in a skillet before stuffing, baking, and serving the chiles in a glass baking dish. To skip the sautéing, microwave the filling in the baking dish first.

Chicken Picadillo—Stuffed Poblanos

MAKES 4 SERVINGS

☀

4 LARGE POBLANO CHILES

2 TABLESPOONS OLIVE OIL

1 MEDIUM ONION, CHOPPED (ABOUT 3/4 CUP)

1 SMALL YELLOW BELL PEPPER, CHOPPED (1 TO 1 1/4 CUPS)

2 LARGE GARLIC CLOVES, CHOPPED (ABOUT 1 TABLESPOON)

1 POUND GROUND CHICKEN

ONE 14 1/2-OUNCE CAN DICED TOMATOES IN JUICE

1/2 CUP SLICED GREEN OLIVES WITH PIMIENTOS

1/3 CUP RAISINS

3/4 TEASPOON GROUND CUMIN

1/4 TEASPOON CINNAMON

4 OUNCES MONTEREY JACK, SHREDDED (ABOUT 1 CUP)

Char the poblano chiles one at a time over a gas burner turned to high heat, turning until all sides are blackened. (Alternatively, heat the broiler. Place the whole chiles on a broiler pan and broil on each side until blackened, 2 to 3 minutes per side.) Place the blackened chiles in a large bowl topped with plastic wrap; let rest for 10 minutes. Remove from the bowl and scrape the blackened skin from the chiles. Cut off the top of each chile and cut down one side from top to bottom. Remove the seeds and membranes.

Heat the oven to 350°F. Grease a 12 × 8-inch glass or ceramic baking dish.

Heat the olive oil in a large skillet over medium-high heat. Add the onion and bell pepper; sauté until softened and beginning to brown, 4 to 5 minutes. Add the garlic; sauté until fragrant, 30 seconds to 1 minute. Add the chicken; cook, stirring constantly and crumbling with a wooden spoon or heatproof spatula, until no longer pink, 4 to 5 minutes. Add the tomatoes with their juice, the olives, raisins, cumin, and cinnamon; reduce the heat to medium and cook, uncovered, until the liquid is evaporated, 7 to 10 minutes. Remove and let cool. Stir in the cheese.

Place one chile in the prepared baking dish; place one-fourth of the filling down the center. Repeat with the remaining chiles, pulling up the sides of the chiles to form a boat shape. Bake for 15 minutes, or until piping hot and the cheese is melted.

MAKE AHEAD Assemble the chiles in the prepared baking dish and refrigerate, covered, until ready to bake. Bake as directed, but allow an extra 5 to 10 minutes for the filling to heat through.

SERVE WITH Beans and rice, if desired, but a simple citrus-dressed salad would do, along with warm tortillas.

Making tamales as individual servings can be a laborious process; preparing them as a single pot pie in a cazuela, a Spanish cooking dish, simplifies the process. I used a 12 × 8-inch glass baking dish, more commonly found in American kitchens, and streamlined this recipe by using prepared salsa verde.

Tamale Cazuela

(Chicken Tamale Pie)

MAKES 8 SERVINGS

✳

FILLING

2½ CUPS COOKED, SHREDDED CHICKEN

1 CUP MEDIUM SALSA VERDE

½ TEASPOON GROUND CUMIN

TAMALE

3 CUPS INSTANT MASA HARINA

2 TEASPOONS BAKING POWDER

3/4 TEASPOON SALT

3/4 CUP VEGETABLE SHORTENING OR LARD, IN PIECES

3 CUPS REDUCED-SODIUM CHICKEN BROTH

2 CUPS SHREDDED CO-JACK CHEESE (OR 1 CUP SHREDDED COLBY AND 1 CUP SHREDDED MONTEREY JACK)

CILANTRO LEAVES

SOUR CREAM

Heat the oven to 350°F. Lightly grease a 12 × 8-inch glass baking dish.

For the filling, stir the chicken, salsa, and cumin together in a medium bowl; set aside.

For the tamale, pulse the masa, baking powder, and salt together in a food processor fitted with a metal blade, using five quick pulses. Add the shortening; pulse to combine, about 15 seconds. Add 2 cups of the chicken broth; process until combined, about 15 seconds. Let the mixture rest for about 1 minute, then add the remaining broth in three batches, processing each until combined, 5 to 10 seconds. The mixture will be soft and fluffy.

Spread half the masa mixture over the bottom of the prepared pan; top with the chicken mixture, leaving a 1-inch border. Spoon the remaining masa over the top. Cover tightly with aluminum foil and bake for 1 hour. Remove the foil; bake for 10 minutes. Sprinkle with the cheese and bake until the cheese is melted and the top of the tamale pie is set, about 10 minutes. Serve the cilantro and sour cream on the side.

MAKE AHEAD Make and bake the pie as directed; refrigerate, covered. Reheat, covered with aluminum foil, in a 350°F oven until heated through, about 30 minutes.

SERVE WITH A tossed green salad with sliced fresh tomatoes, avocado, and radishes.

*E*verything—the chicken, carrots, and potatoes—bakes together with a vinegar-based marinade that's enhanced by a healthy dose of soy sauce. The result is a richly browned and deeply flavored one-pan oven meal.

Philippine Chicken Adobo

MAKES 4 SERVINGS

✳

1/3 CUP CIDER VINEGAR

4 LARGE GARLIC CLOVES,
COARSELY CHOPPED
(ABOUT 2 TABLESPOONS)

2 BAY LEAVES

1/4 TEASPOON PLUS
1/8 TEASPOON COARSE, FRESHLY
GROUND PEPPER

4 BONE-IN, SKIN-ON CHICKEN
BREAST HALVES

4 MEDIUM CARROTS, PEELED
AND CUT IN 1 1/2-INCH CHUNKS

4 MEDIUM-SMALL RED BOILING
POTATOES (ABOUT 1 POUND),
PEELED AND CUT IN HALVES OR
QUARTERS

1/4 CUP SOY SAUCE

1/4 TEASPOON SALT

Combine the cider vinegar, garlic, bay leaves, and 1/4 teaspoon pepper in a 1-gallon self-sealing plastic bag. Squeeze to blend. Add the chicken; seal, then turn and squeeze to coat the chicken. Marinate for 30 minutes at room temperature.

Meanwhile, heat the oven to 400°F. Remove the chicken and arrange, skin side up, in a single layer in a shallow, nonreactive metal roasting pan just slightly larger than the chicken pieces. Pour the marinade over the chicken and bake for 10 minutes. Scatter the carrots and potatoes around the chicken. Pour the soy sauce over all; season with the salt and the remaining 1/8 teaspoon pepper. Bake for an additional 40 to 45 minutes, basting occasionally with the pan juices, until the chicken is no longer pink in the thickest portion when cut with a knife.

Arrange an oven rack 5 to 6 inches from the broiler. Heat the broiler while removing the chicken, carrots, and potatoes from the pan; pour off the pan juices. Return the chicken, skin side up, the carrots, and potatoes to the pan. Place under the broiler until the chicken is a deep brown and the skin is crisp, 2 to 3 minutes. Remove and serve. Skim the surface fat from the pan juices and serve the juices alongside.

MAKE AHEAD Finish the recipe up to the point of broiling. Refrigerate, covered. Reheat, tented with aluminum foil, in a 350°F oven until just warmed through, 20 to 30 minutes. Proceed as directed.

SERVE WITH A tossed salad with tomatoes plus crusty bread.

ecause Thai chickens tend to be smaller than American birds, using Cornish hens is a logical substitute. This marinade is typically used for barbecued chicken, but makes a great sauce when poured over the hens. Add the sweet potatoes, onion, and bell peppers before popping everything in the oven.

Thai Cornish Game Hens

MAKES 4 SERVINGS

✳

1 CUP COCONUT MILK

1 CUP CHOPPED CILANTRO

1/3 CUP COARSELY CHOPPED LEMONGRASS, TENDER PORTIONS ONLY

1 JALAPEÑO, CHOPPED

1/4 CUP CHOPPED SHALLOTS

4 LARGE GARLIC CLOVES, CHOPPED (ABOUT 2 TABLESPOONS)

2 TABLESPOONS NAM PLA (FISH SAUCE)

2 TABLESPOONS BROWN SUGAR

2 TABLESPOONS LIME JUICE

1 TABLESPOON CHOPPED GINGER

1 TABLESPOON SOY SAUCE

2 CORNISH GAME HENS, HALVED LENGTHWISE

2 SWEET POTATOES, YAMS, OR RED GARNET YAMS, PEELED, QUARTERED LENGTHWISE, AND CUT IN 1 1/2-INCH PIECES

1 LARGE RED ONION, QUARTERED AND CUT IN 1-INCH WEDGES

1 GREEN BELL PEPPER, CUT IN 1-INCH PIECES

1 RED BELL PEPPER, CUT IN 1-INCH PIECES

Combine the coconut milk, cilantro, lemongrass, jalapeño, shallots, garlic, nam pla, brown sugar, lime juice, ginger, and soy sauce in a 1-gallon self-sealing plastic bag; squeeze to blend. Add the Cornish hens; turn and squeeze to coat. Marinate for 1 hour at room temperature.

Meanwhile, heat the oven to 375°F. Scatter the sweet potatoes, onion, and green and red bell peppers over the bottom of a large roasting pan.

When the hens are marinated, arrange them, skin side up, on top of the vegetables. Pour the marinade over all and bake, basting occasionally, until the hens are no longer pink in the thickest portion of the thigh when cut with a knife, about 45 minutes.

MAKE AHEAD Assemble all the marinade ingredients in the bag and refrigerate until ready to proceed with the recipe.

SERVE WITH Jasmine or basmati rice is an excellent accompaniment for soaking up the sauce. Sliced cucumbers, topped with peanuts and drizzled with a bit of rice vinegar, fish sauce, and sugar stirred together, would make a nice side salad.

6 Skillet Meals

I will always associate this recipe with my aunt Lucille; it was a favorite of her generation, and she successfully served it at many a ladies' luncheon. And with just reason. Creamy bits of chicken float over crisp bits of puff pastry shaped into a patty shell or—as the French would put it—a vol-au-vent.

Chicken à la King

※

4 TABLESPOONS (1/2 STICK)
SALTED BUTTER

1 TABLESPOON CANOLA OIL

1/4 CUP CHOPPED SHALLOTS

1/2 CUP CHOPPED
RED BELL PEPPER

8 OUNCES WHITE BUTTON
MUSHROOMS, SLICED

1/2 TEASPOON SALT

1/4 TEASPOON FRESHLY
GROUND PEPPER

2 TABLESPOONS CHOPPED
FRESH TARRAGON

1/4 CUP ALL-PURPOSE FLOUR

ONE 14-OUNCE CAN
REDUCED-SODIUM
CHICKEN BROTH

2 TABLESPOONS SHERRY

1/4 CUP CRÈME FRAÎCHE

3 CUPS COOKED, DICED
CHICKEN

6 BAKED PUFF PASTRY
PATTY SHELLS

Heat 1 tablespoon of the butter and the canola oil in a large skillet over medium heat. When sizzling, add the shallots; sauté for 1 minute. Add the bell pepper; sauté for an additional minute. Add the mushrooms, 1/4 teaspoon of the salt, and 1/8 teaspoon of the pepper; increase the heat to medium-high. Sauté until the mushrooms are softened, 3 to 4 minutes; stir in 1 tablespoon of the tarragon. Remove and set aside.

Melt the remaining 3 tablespoons butter in the same skillet over medium heat; stir in the flour. Cook for 2 minutes, stirring constantly. Whisk in the chicken broth until smooth; bring to a boil, stirring often. Whisk in the sherry. Reduce the heat to medium-low; cook for 2 minutes. Whisk in the crème fraîche. Stir in the cooked chicken and the mushroom mixture; season with the remaining 1/4 teaspoon salt and 1/8 teaspoon pepper. Spoon over the baked puff pastry patty shells; sprinkle each serving with 1/2 teaspoon of the remaining tarragon.

MAKE AHEAD Make the sauce for the chicken mixture through adding the crème fraîche. Refrigerate the sauce, the cooked chicken, and the mushroom mixture separately, covered. When ready to serve, heat the mixture over low heat until simmering, then stir in the chicken and the mushroom mixture, season, and proceed as directed.

SERVE WITH A nicely garnished fresh fruit plate on the side, Parker House rolls, and tall glasses of iced tea.

*L*ike peach Melba, chicken Tetrazzini, invented by an American restaurateur, gets its name from a renowned female opera singer of the time, in this case Luisa Tetrazzini. Made with noodles, the dish has a pleasantly satisfying richness without being overwhelmingly heavy.

Chicken Tetrazzini

Heat the canola oil in a large skillet over medium heat. Add the shallots; sauté until just softened, stirring occasionally, 3 to 4 minutes. Add the mushrooms; toss with the lemon juice. Sauté until softened, 5 to 8 minutes. Season with the salt, 1/8 teaspoon of the pepper, and the cayenne. Remove to a medium bowl.

Melt the butter in the skillet over medium-low heat. Whisk in the flour; cook for 2 minutes, whisking constantly. Whisk in the chicken broth, milk, nutmeg, and remaining 1/8 teaspoon pepper until smooth. Increase the heat to medium-high; bring to a boil. Boil until thickened, about 2 minutes. Stir in the mushrooms, chicken, noodles, and 2/3 cup of the Parmesan. Top with the remaining 1/3 cup Parmesan and the almonds. Serve.

MAKE AHEAD Complete the recipe up to topping with the final 1/3 cup Parmesan and the almonds and refrigerate, covered. When ready to serve, bake in a 375°F oven, covered with aluminum foil, for 35 to 40 minutes, or until heated through. Remove the foil; sprinkle with the remaining Parmesan and the almonds.

SERVE WITH A tossed salad with torn bits of fresh basil plus crusty dinner rolls.

*F*luffy buttermilk biscuits top a medley of chicken and vegetables, baked and served in a cast-iron frying pan. If you don't have this old-fashioned treasure, start with a large skillet and then use a deep-dish pie plate for baking. Sweet potato subs for the more standard white variety, adding an extra hit of color, taste, and vitamins.

MAKES 4 TO 6 SERVINGS

✳

CHICKEN FILLING

2 TABLESPOONS CANOLA OIL

1 MEDIUM ONION, CHOPPED
(ABOUT 3/4 CUP)

6 BONELESS, SKINLESS CHICKEN
THIGHS, CUT IN 1-INCH CUBES

1/4 CUP ALL-PURPOSE FLOUR

1 CUP REDUCED-SODIUM
CHICKEN BROTH

1/4 CUP WHITE WINE

1/2 MEDIUM SWEET POTATO,
PEELED AND CUT IN 1/2-INCH
DICE (ABOUT 3/4 CUP)

1 MEDIUM CARROT,
PEELED AND CUT IN 1/2-INCH
DICE (ABOUT 1/2 CUP)

1 LARGE CELERY STALK, CUT IN
1/2-INCH DICE (ABOUT 1/2 CUP)

1/2 CUP SHELLED FRESH PEAS
(OR FROZEN AND THAWED)

1/2 CUP FRESH CORN KERNELS
(OR FROZEN AND THAWED)

3/4 TEASPOON DRIED
THYME

1/4 TEASPOON SALT

1/8 TEASPOON FRESHLY
GROUND PEPPER

Chicken and Biscuit Pie

For the filling, heat the canola oil in a 10-inch cast-iron frying pan (or a large skillet) over medium-high heat; add the onion. Sauté for 2 minutes; add the chicken. Sauté until the chicken is no longer pink on the outside, stirring frequently, an additional 4 to 5 minutes. Sprinkle with the flour and stir to blend. Stir in the chicken broth and white wine until well blended. Bring to a simmer; reduce the heat to medium-low and add the sweet potato, carrot, and celery. Cook, uncovered, until the carrot is crisp-tender, 15 to 20 minutes. Gently stir in the peas, corn, thyme, salt, and pepper. (If using a large skillet, pour the mixture into a deep-dish 9-inch pie plate.)

Meanwhile, heat the oven to 425°F.

For the biscuits, cut the flour and butter together until the mixture resembles coarse meal in a medium mixing bowl. Stir in the buttermilk a little at a time until the dough is just mixed. The dough will be very soft. Drop the dough in heaping tablespoons over the top of the filling so that the mounds are just touching. Bake for 25 minutes, until the biscuits are browned and the filling is bubbly.

MAKE AHEAD Make the filling for the pie and refrigerate, covered, until ready to bake. Reheat the filling in the frying pan (or pour it, reheated, into the pie plate). Proceed with the recipe as directed.

SERVE WITH A crisp tossed salad.

BISCUIT CRUST

1¹/₂ CUPS SELF-RISING FLOUR, PREFERABLY WHITE LILY

3 TABLESPOONS CHILLED SALTED BUTTER, CUT IN PIECES

¹/₂ TO ²/₃ CUP BUTTERMILK

I make my pot pies with a single, top crust only. That way I can concentrate on using a flaky, rich pastry and not worry about making a sturdier crust for the bottom that will hold up to the liquid in the filling. This crust is made particularly rich with the addition of Cheddar.

Once again, if you don't have an ovenproof skillet, make the filling, then transfer it to a deep-dish pie pan for baking.

✳

CRUST

1 CUP ALL-PURPOSE FLOUR

1/4 TEASPOON SALT

6 TABLESPOONS CHILLED UNSALTED BUTTER, CUT IN 1/2-INCH DICE

2/3 CUP LIGHTLY PACKED, GRATED HIGH-QUALITY AMERICAN CHEDDAR

2 TABLESPOONS CHOPPED FRESH CHIVES

FILLING

2 TABLESPOONS SALTED BUTTER

1/4 CUP ALL-PURPOSE FLOUR

1 1/2 CUPS REDUCED-SODIUM CHICKEN BROTH

1/4 TEASPOON SALT

1/8 TEASPOON FRESHLY GROUND PEPPER

1 CUP FROZEN PEARL ONIONS, THAWED

1 LARGE CARROT, PEELED AND CUT IN 3/4-INCH DICE (ABOUT 3/4 CUP)

2 CUPS BROCCOLI FLORETS

2 CUPS COOKED, DICED CHICKEN

Skillet Chicken Pot Pie

For the crust, stir the flour and salt together in a medium bowl. Cut in the butter until the mixture resembles coarse crumbs. Stir in the cheese and chives. Toss with enough ice water to form a ball, 2 to 3 tablespoons; flatten into a disk and wrap with plastic wrap. Refrigerate while preparing the filling.

Heat the oven to 400°F.

For the filling, melt the butter in an ovenproof 10-inch skillet over medium-low heat. Whisk in the flour and cook for 2 minutes, stirring constantly. Whisk in the chicken broth, salt, and pepper until no lumps remain. Increase the heat to medium and bring to a boil. Add the onions and carrot and bring back to a boil. Reduce the heat to medium-low and cook, uncovered, for 10 minutes, stirring occasionally. Add the broccoli and cook, covered, for 10 minutes. Remove from the heat and stir in the chicken.

Roll out the chilled dough on a floured surface to an 11-inch circle. Cover the skillet with the dough, pinching the overlapping dough along the edge of the skillet to form a border. Crimp against the sides of the skillet with a fork if desired. Bake for 15 minutes, or until the crust is browned.

MAKE AHEAD   Have the filling made and kept, covered, in the refrigerator and have the crust ready to roll out. Reheat the filling before baking and then top with the crust.

SERVE WITH   A green salad tossed with a mustard vinaigrette and garnished with walnuts.

ot four-and-twenty blackbirds, but moist and tender chicken thighs are baked into this pie, enhanced with sliced green olives and capers, and topped with an egg yolk–enriched piecrust that duplicates empanada dough. Once again, the recipe has only a top crust to eliminate any worries over a soggy bottom pastry.

Puerto Rican Empanada Pie

MAKES 4 SERVINGS

❋

2 TABLESPOONS OLIVE OIL

1 LARGE ONION, CHOPPED (ABOUT 1½ CUPS)

1 GREEN BELL PEPPER, CHOPPED (ABOUT 1½ CUPS)

⅓ CUP DICED HAM

2 LARGE GARLIC CLOVES, CHOPPED (ABOUT 1 TABLESPOON)

6 BONELESS, SKINLESS CHICKEN THIGHS, CUT IN 1-INCH CUBES

ONE 14½-OUNCE CAN DICED TOMATOES IN JUICE

⅓ CUP SLICED GREEN OLIVES WITH PIMIENTOS

1 TABLESPOON NONPAREIL CAPERS (IN VINEGAR), RINSED

1 TEASPOON FINELY GRATED ORANGE ZEST

¼ TEASPOON FRESHLY GROUND PEPPER

3 SMALL RED POTATOES (ABOUT ½ POUND), PEELED AND CUT IN ½-INCH CUBES

1 TABLESPOON CORNMEAL

For the filling, heat the olive oil in a 10-inch ovenproof skillet over medium heat (or use a large skillet and transfer the mixture before baking to a deep-dish pie pan). Add the onion and bell pepper; sauté until beginning to soften, 3 to 4 minutes. Add the ham; sauté for 2 minutes. Add the garlic; sauté until fragrant, 30 seconds to 1 minute. Add the chicken; sauté until lightly browned, turning occasionally, 5 to 6 minutes. Add the tomatoes with their juice, the olives, capers, orange zest, and pepper. Stir to blend. Add the potatoes and stir again. Bring just to a boil; reduce the heat to medium-low and cook, covered, for 10 minutes. Remove the cover; stir and cook for an additional 15 minutes. Stir in the cornmeal; cook until thickened, about 5 minutes.

Meanwhile, heat the oven to 425°F.

For the crust, mix the flour and salt together in a medium bowl. Cut in the butter until the mixture is the texture of coarse sand with some pebbles. Whisk the egg yolk, white wine, and 2 tablespoons water together in a small bowl. Stir into the flour mixture just until it forms a ball. Roll the dough out into a 10-inch circle on a lightly floured counter.

When the chicken mixture is thickened, top with the circle of dough; trim the edges and bake for 15 minutes, or until the crust is lightly browned. Remove; cut the crust into wedges and serve the pie.

MAKE AHEAD Make the filling and refrigerate, covered. Make the dough; shape it into a disk and wrap it in plastic wrap. Refrigerate until ready to bake; then roll the disk into a 10-inch circle. Reheat the filling before baking; top with the circle of dough and bake as directed.

SERVE WITH A crisp salad, tossed with a lime and olive oil vinaigrette.

CRUST

1¼ CUPS ALL-PURPOSE FLOUR

¼ TEASPOON SALT

6 TABLESPOONS CHILLED UNSALTED BUTTER, CUT IN ½-INCH DICE

1 LARGE EGG YOLK

1 TABLESPOON WHITE WINE (OR LEMON JUICE)

*E*ngland has a tradition of pub food—satisfying meals that are the essence of eating. Pour a pint, settle next to a crackling fire, and serve a piping-hot portion of shepherd's pie for a bit of the British Isles right at home.

Chicken Shepherd's Pie

MAKES 4 SERVINGS

❊

2 TABLESPOONS CANOLA OIL

2 MEDIUM LEEKS, WHITE AND
PALE GREEN PORTIONS,
TRIMMED, HALVED,
THOROUGHLY RINSED, AND
CHOPPED (ABOUT 1¹/₂ CUPS)

4 BONELESS, SKINLESS
CHICKEN THIGHS, CUT IN BITE-
SIZED PIECES

¹/₄ TEASPOON SALT

¹/₄ TEASPOON FRESHLY
GROUND PEPPER

2 MEDIUM CARROTS, PEELED
AND CHOPPED (ABOUT 1 CUP)

³/₄ TEASPOON POULTRY
SEASONING

¹/₂ TEASPOON DRIED,
RUBBED SAGE

¹/₃ CUP PLUS ¹/₄ CUP
REDUCED-SODIUM
CHICKEN BROTH

¹/₃ CUP WHITE WINE

1 TABLESPOON CORNSTARCH

2¹/₂ TO 3 CUPS
MASHED POTATOES

¹/₄ CUP FRESHLY GRATED
PARMIGIANO-REGGIANO

Heat the canola oil in a medium ovenproof skillet over medium heat; add the leeks. Sauté until beginning to brown, 4 to 5 minutes; add the chicken, seasoned with the salt and ¹/8 teaspoon of the pepper. Sauté until beginning to brown, stirring often, 4 to 5 minutes. Add the carrots, poultry seasoning, and sage; stir to blend. Add the ¹/₃ cup chicken broth and the white wine; bring just to a boil.

Reduce the heat to low and cook, partially covered, for 20 minutes. Stir the remaining ¹/₄ cup chicken broth and the cornstarch together in a small bowl; stir into the chicken mixture and cook until thickened, 2 to 3 minutes. Remove from the heat.

Meanwhile, heat the oven to 425°F.

Stir the remaining ¹/8 teaspoon pepper into the potatoes; spoon the potatoes over the top of the chicken mixture in the skillet. Sprinkle with the Parmesan. Bake until bubbling and just beginning to brown, 15 to 20 minutes.

MAKE AHEAD This recipe can be prepared up to baking in the oven. Refrigerate the filling, covered, until ready to reheat. Heat the mixture over medium-low heat until simmering, stir in the pepper, and bake, topped with the potatoes as directed.

SERVE WITH A simple salad tossed with a mustard vinaigrette plus multigrain rolls to make this cozy meal complete.

The hills in our part of Provence produce more than wine, olives, and lavender, as if those were not enough. Apricot trees are scattered in patches throughout this portion of France, blossoming in the spring in a glorious promise of the nectared fruit yet to come. Once harvested, the apricots take their turn in the market stalls, first fresh and succulent, then as concentrated dried fruit. A local distillery makes an apricot eau-de-vie that captures their very essence in a bottle.

Using these elements for inspiration, I've come up with this quickly prepared but elegant single-skillet main course that reminds me of my French countryside when I'm home in the States.

Apricot Chicken

MAKES 4 SERVINGS

❊

1 TABLESPOON OLIVE OIL

1 TABLESPOON SALTED BUTTER

1/4 CUP CHOPPED SHALLOTS

FOUR 6-OUNCE BONELESS, SKINLESS CHICKEN BREAST HALVES

1 1/2 TEASPOONS HERBES DE PROVENCE

1/4 TEASPOON SALT

1/8 TEASPOON FRESHLY GROUND PEPPER

1/4 CUP APRICOT BRANDY (OR COGNAC)

3/4 CUP REDUCED-SODIUM CHICKEN BROTH

1/2 CUP WHITE WINE

1/2 CUP CHOPPED DRIED APRICOTS

1 TABLESPOON LEMON JUICE

Heat the olive oil and butter in a large skillet over medium heat. When sizzling, add the shallots; sauté for 2 minutes. Add the chicken, seasoned with the herbes de Provence, salt, and pepper; sauté until golden brown, about 3 minutes per side. Add the apricot brandy; ignite.

When the flames subside, add the chicken broth, white wine, apricots, and lemon juice. Reduce the heat to low; cover and cook for 5 minutes. Turn and cook, covered, until the chicken is no longer pink in the thickest portion when cut with a knife, an additional 4 to 5 minutes. Remove the chicken to a platter.

Increase the heat to high and boil until the liquid is reduced by about one-third, 2 to 3 minutes. Pour the pan sauce and apricots over the chicken; serve.

MAKE AHEAD Have everything chopped and measured in advance, then prepare before serving.

SERVE WITH Basmati rice and a simple salad. If you wish, add the thin green beans known as *haricots verts*.

Inspired by a quick sauté of pork I ate at the restaurant and cooking school Zeppelin in Orvieto, Italy, I've chosen the original white meat—chicken—for my version of this dish. True to its origins, it is simple yet packed with flavor. In Italy, as a main course, it could easily be served without accompaniment, but the suggestions I've included at the end help to round out the meal for American diners.

Chicken Zeppelin

MAKES 4 SERVINGS

❄

2 TABLESPOONS OLIVE OIL

FOUR 6- TO 8-OUNCE
BONELESS, SKINLESS CHICKEN
BREAST HALVES

1/2 TEASPOON SALT

1/4 TEASPOON FRESHLY
GROUND PEPPER

3 LARGE GARLIC CLOVES,
CHOPPED (ABOUT
1 1/2 TABLESPOONS)

1 TABLESPOON MINCED
FRESH ROSEMARY

1/4 CUP BALSAMIC VINEGAR

3/4 CUP WHITE WINE

Heat the olive oil in a large skillet over medium-high heat. Add the chicken, seasoned with the salt and pepper. Sauté until browned, 3 to 4 minutes per side. Sprinkle with half of the garlic and rosemary; turn and season the other side with the remaining garlic and rosemary.

Reduce the heat to medium-low; sauté for 3 minutes. Turn; pour the balsamic vinegar over the chicken. Sauté for an additional 2 minutes. Turn; pour the white wine over the chicken breasts. Continue cooking until the chicken is no longer pink in the thickest portion when cut with a knife, an additional 3 to 4 minutes per side. Serve with some of the sauce spooned over the top of each breast.

MAKE AHEAD Have all the ingredients premeasured and chopped.

SERVE WITH Roasted potatoes and artichokes or peas.

*T*he Greeks do wonderful things with chicken as this recipe attests. Here, breast meat is stuffed with feta and quickly cooked in a skillet. Then, in the same pan, a bit of red wine and cinnamon transforms the pan juices into a magical sauce.

Chicken with Red Wine, Raisins, and Onions

Toss the feta and oregano together in a small bowl. Press the tenderloin flap outward on each chicken breast, leaving it attached. Cut a 3-inch wide pocket halfway through the thickness of each breast, centering the cut and cutting horizontally toward the thicker side. Cut until the pocket reaches to about 1/2 inch from the thickest side. (If the breasts come without a tenderloin, butterfly a small section of the breast along the thinner rib side to form a flap for folding over the pocket.) Stuff each breast with one-fourth of the feta mixture. Tuck the top edge of each pocket inward and fold the tenderloin edge over the pocket like the flap of an envelope. Tuck the bottom point of the breast upward. Seal the edges securely closed with toothpicks; season with the salt and pepper.

Heat the olive oil in a large skillet over medium-high heat. Add the breasts, sealed side down; sauté until browned, 3 to 4 minutes. Turn and sauté for 2 minutes; add the onions and sauté for an additional 2 minutes, stirring the onions occasionally to prevent scorching. Add the chicken broth and raisins; reduce the heat to low and cook, covered, until the chicken is no longer pink when cut at the thickest portion of the unstuffed top of the breast, 8 to 10 minutes. Remove the chicken to a platter; cover with aluminum foil to keep warm. *(continued)*

Add the red wine and cinnamon to the skillet and increase the heat to high; boil to reduce the liquid by half, 3 to 4 minutes. Pour over the chicken; serve.

MAKE AHEAD The chicken breasts can be stuffed and refrigerated, covered, until ready to cook. Have all the other ingredients organized ahead of time.

SERVE WITH Sugar snap peas or green beans along with your choice of rice, orzo, or roasted potatoes.

*A*dd some calypso music in the background, serve up chicken laced with rum and lime, and the Caribbean is as close as your dinner table.

Calypso Chicken

MAKES 4 SERVINGS

❋

1 TABLESPOON OLIVE OIL

8 BONE-IN, SKIN-ON
CHICKEN THIGHS

$^{1}/_{2}$ TEASPOON SALT

$^{1}/_{4}$ TEASPOON FRESHLY
GROUND PEPPER

1 LARGE ONION, CHOPPED
(ABOUT 1$^{1}/_{2}$ CUPS)

1 RED BELL PEPPER, CHOPPED
(ABOUT 1$^{1}/_{2}$ CUPS)

1 LARGE GARLIC CLOVE,
CHOPPED (ABOUT
1$^{1}/_{2}$ TEASPOONS)

1$^{1}/_{2}$ TEASPOONS
CHOPPED GINGER

1 CUP MEDIUM-GRAIN RICE

ONE 14-OUNCE CAN
REDUCED-SODIUM
CHICKEN BROTH

$^{1}/_{3}$ CUP LIGHT RUM

2 TABLESPOONS LIME JUICE

1 TEASPOON FINELY GRATED
LIME ZEST

$^{1}/_{8}$ TEASPOON HABAÑERO OR
CARIBBEAN-STYLE HOT SAUCE

Heat the olive oil in a large skillet over medium-high heat. Add the chicken in batches, seasoned with the salt and pepper, skin side down, and sauté until browned, 3 to 4 minutes. Turn and sauté the other side until browned, 3 to 4 minutes. Remove the chicken and drain off all but 2 tablespoons of the fat. Add the onion and bell pepper; sauté until softened, 3 to 4 minutes. Add the garlic and ginger; sauté until fragrant, 30 seconds to 1 minute. Stir in the rice; sauté, stirring occasionally, for 2 minutes. Add the chicken broth, rum, lime juice, lime zest, and habañero sauce; stir to blend. Return the chicken to the skillet, skin side up. Bring just to a boil; reduce the heat to low and cook, covered, stirring once after 15 minutes, until the chicken is no longer pink when cut in the thickest portion with a knife, the rice is tender, and all the liquid has been absorbed, about 30 minutes.

MAKE AHEAD Complete the recipe and refrigerate, covered. Before serving, let the chicken and rice rest at room temperature for an hour. Transfer to a microwave-safe container and microwave on high power, stirring occasionally, until piping hot.

SERVE WITH The tropical drink of your choice, then add an orange-topped salad and corn muffins as accompaniments.

*J*ambalaya makes me smile. The word itself sounds like a party, and the finished product lives up to its name. Made zesty with andouille sausages, Cajun seasoning, and a splash of Louisiana's own Tabasco, this New Orleans version of paella lets the good times roll.

Chicken Jambalaya

MAKES 6 SERVINGS

✳

1 TABLESPOON CANOLA OIL

3 BONE-IN, SKIN-ON CHICKEN BREAST HALVES, CUT IN HALF ACROSS THE BONE

3 BONE-IN, SKIN-ON CHICKEN THIGHS

3 BONE-IN, SKIN-ON CHICKEN DRUMSTICKS

1/2 TEASPOON SALT

1/4 TEASPOON GROUND WHITE PEPPER

1/4 TEASPOON FRESHLY GROUND BLACK PEPPER

4 ANDOUILLE SAUSAGES, CUT IN THIRDS

1 LARGE ONION, CHOPPED (ABOUT 1 1/2 CUPS)

1 GREEN BELL PEPPER, CHOPPED (ABOUT 1 1/2 CUPS)

2 LARGE CELERY STALKS, CHOPPED (ABOUT 1 CUP)

2 LARGE GARLIC CLOVES, MINCED (ABOUT 1 TABLESPOON)

ONE 14 1/2-OUNCE CAN DICED TOMATOES IN JUICE

ONE 14-OUNCE CAN REDUCED-SODIUM CHICKEN BROTH

Heat the canola oil over medium-high heat in a large, deep skillet. Add the chicken in batches, seasoned with the salt, white pepper, and black pepper; sauté until browned, 3 to 4 minutes per side. Remove.

Add the sausage pieces to the skillet; sauté until browned on all sides, 4 to 5 minutes total. Remove.

Add the onion, bell pepper, and celery; reduce the heat to medium-low. Sauté until the onion is softened, 6 to 8 minutes. Stir in the garlic; sauté until fragrant, 30 seconds to 1 minute. Add the tomatoes and their juice; return the chicken and sausage to the skillet. Reduce the heat to low and cook, partially covered, for 20 minutes.

Remove the chicken. Add the chicken broth, Cajun seasoning, and Tabasco sauce; increase the heat to medium. Bring to a boil; stir in the rice. Boil for 5 minutes; stir.

Reduce the heat to low; return the chicken to the pan. Cook, covered, until the chicken is no longer pink in the thickest portion when cut with a knife and the rice is tender, 20 to 25 minutes.

MAKE AHEAD To make the jambalaya ahead, the best method is to substitute 12 bone-in, skin-on chicken thighs for all the chicken pieces. Instead of cooking the chicken and sausage for only 20 minutes initially, cook the thighs until completely done, 40 to 45 minutes, stirring occasionally to keep from scorching. Then refrigerate the mixture, covered. When ready, remove the chicken; add the broth, Cajun seasoning, and Tabasco and bring to a boil. Proceed with the recipe as written.

SERVE WITH Baking powder biscuits and a fresh green salad tossed with buttermilk dressing.

1^1/$_2$ TEASPOONS CAJUN
SEASONING

^{1}/$_4$ TEASPOON TABASCO SAUCE

1^1/$_2$ CUPS CONVERTED RICE

Étouffée, or smothered, chicken is a Louisiana specialty, incorporating the classic vegetable trinity—onion, peppers, and celery—in a zesty covering for the bird below. Corn kernels add extra color and a note of sweetness, acting as a foil for the spicy-salty Cajun seasoning.

Chicken Étouffée

MAKES 4 SERVINGS

❋

3 TABLESPOONS SALTED BUTTER

1 LARGE ONION, CHOPPED (ABOUT 1½ CUPS)

3 MEDIUM CELERY STALKS, CHOPPED (ABOUT 1 CUP)

1 RED BELL PEPPER, CHOPPED (ABOUT 1½ CUPS)

1 GREEN BELL PEPPER, CHOPPED (ABOUT 1½ CUPS)

2 TEASPOONS CAJUN SEASONING

⅛ TEASPOON CAYENNE

ONE 3½- TO 4-POUND CHICKEN, CUT IN PIECES

1 TABLESPOON CANOLA OIL

1 CUP FRESH CORN KERNELS (OR FROZEN AND THAWED)

Melt the butter in a large skillet over medium-low heat. Add the onion and celery; sauté until soft and translucent, 8 to 10 minutes. Add the red and green bell peppers; sauté until beginning to soften, 4 to 5 minutes. Season with 1 teaspoon of the Cajun seasoning and the cayenne; remove to a bowl.

Season the chicken with the remaining 1 teaspoon Cajun seasoning. Heat the canola oil in the same skillet over medium-high heat. Sauté the chicken, in batches if necessary, until browned, 3 to 4 minutes per side. Cover the chicken with the onion mixture; reduce the heat to low. Cook, covered, until the chicken is no longer pink in the thickest portion when cut with a knife, 35 to 45 minutes. Sprinkle with the corn and cook, covered, for an additional 5 minutes.

MAKE AHEAD Complete the recipe up to adding the corn; refrigerate, covered, until ready to serve. Then reheat, covered, over low heat, until the chicken is warmed through. Add a splash of water, if necessary, to keep the mixture from scorching. Add the corn and cook, covered, for 5 minutes.

SERVE WITH Basmati rice and sliced tomatoes.

*L*ike its Spanish cousin, arroz con pollo, this Cuban recipe cooks chicken together with rice in a wonderfully symbiotic combination. Annatto, or achiote, seeds add a rich tint as an alternative to saffron. When buying the seeds, make sure they are a rust color and not old and brown.

MAKES 4 SERVINGS

✻

2 TABLESPOONS OLIVE OIL

1 TABLESPOON ANNATTO
(ACHIOTE) SEEDS

1 LARGE ONION, CHOPPED
(ABOUT 1$^{1}/_{2}$ CUPS)

1 RED BELL PEPPER, CHOPPED
(ABOUT 1$^{1}/_{2}$ CUPS)

2 LARGE GARLIC CLOVES,
CHOPPED (ABOUT
1 TABLESPOON)

1 MEDIUM ROMA TOMATO,
CHOPPED (ABOUT $^{1}/_{3}$ CUP)

1 TEASPOON GROUND CUMIN

$^{1}/_{2}$ TEASPOON DRIED OREGANO,
PREFERABLY MEXICAN

6 BONELESS, SKINLESS CHICKEN
THIGHS, CUT IN HALF

$^{1}/_{2}$ TEASPOON SALT

$^{1}/_{4}$ TEASPOON FRESHLY
GROUND PEPPER

$^{1}/_{2}$ CUP WHITE WINE

1$^{1}/_{2}$ CUPS REDUCED-SODIUM
CHICKEN BROTH

ONE 8-OUNCE PACKAGE
SAFFRON YELLOW RICE

$^{1}/_{2}$ CUP SLICED GREEN OLIVES
WITH PIMIENTOS

1 CUP FROZEN BABY PEAS

$^{1}/_{4}$ CUP CILANTRO LEAVES

Cuban Chicken

Spoon the olive oil into the center of a large skillet and add the annatto seeds to the oil. Turn the heat to the lowest setting; gently cook the seeds in the oil for 5 minutes. Remove from the heat; let the seeds steep for an additional 5 minutes. Pour the mixture into a small dish; strain the oil back into the skillet and discard the seeds.

Increase the heat to medium and add the onion and bell pepper; sauté until the onion is softened, 4 to 5 minutes. Add the garlic; sauté until fragrant, 30 seconds to 1 minute. Stir in the tomato; cook for 1 minute. Stir in the cumin and oregano. Add the chicken, seasoned with the salt and pepper; sauté on each side for 4 minutes. Pour in the white wine and reduce the heat to low; cook, partially covered, for 5 minutes. Turn the chicken; cook for an additional 5 minutes. Remove the cover; pour in the chicken broth and increase the heat to medium. When just beginning to boil, stir in the yellow rice. Reduce the heat again to low; cover and cook for 15 minutes, stirring once or twice. Stir in the olives; sprinkle the peas over the top. Continue to cook until the rice is tender and all the liquid is absorbed, about 10 minutes. Garnish with the cilantro leaves and serve immediately.

MAKE AHEAD Prepare the dish through cooking the chicken in white wine on both sides, but continue cooking until the chicken is no longer pink in the thickest portion when cut with a knife. Refrigerate, covered, and return the mixture to the skillet when ready to serve. Add about $1/4$ cup water and reheat. Add the chicken broth and proceed as directed.

SERVE WITH An avocado and grapefruit–topped salad and crusty bread.

*D*emonstrating that similar ingredients combine across cultures to produce widely divergent results, this northern Indian meal also combines rice, chicken, and seasonings in one cooking vessel. To achieve its unique taste, it uses garam masala. This spice blend, now available in many mainstream grocery stores, consists of an assortment of seasonings, including cinnamon, cloves, black pepper, cumin, and cardamom. Biryanis characteristically contain raisins and nuts as well.

Chicken Biryani

MAKES 4 TO 6 SERVINGS

❋

1 CUP BASMATI RICE

1 LARGE RED ONION

3 TABLESPOONS CANOLA OIL

2 SERRANO CHILES, CHOPPED
(SEEDED, IF DESIRED)

2 LARGE GARLIC CLOVES,
MINCED (ABOUT 1 TABLESPOON)

1 TABLESPOON MINCED GINGER

2 TEASPOONS GARAM MASALA

1 1/2 TEASPOONS
GROUND CUMIN

2 LARGE ROMA TOMATOES,
CHOPPED (ABOUT 1 CUP)

1/2 CUP CRÈME FRAÎCHE

5 TO 6 BONELESS, SKINLESS
CHICKEN THIGHS, CUT IN HALF

1 1/4 TEASPOONS SALT

2 CINNAMON STICKS

1/4 TEASPOON
GROUND CARDAMOM

PINCH SAFFRON THREADS

1/2 CUP GOLDEN RAISINS

1/2 CUP ROASTED CASHEWS

1/4 CUP CHOPPED
CILANTRO LEAVES

1/4 CUP CHOPPED FRESH MINT

Soak the basmati rice in cold water in a medium bowl. Cut the onion in half lengthwise. Chop half the onion; slice the other half and set the slices aside. Heat 1 tablespoon of the canola oil over medium heat in a large, round heatproof gratin dish, paella pan, or a skillet. Add the chopped onion; sauté until lightly browned, about 5 minutes. Stir in the serrano chiles, garlic, ginger, garam masala, and 1 teaspoon of the cumin; sauté until fragrant, 30 seconds to 1 minute. Stir in the tomatoes; reduce the heat to medium-low and simmer for 4 minutes. Stir in the crème fraîche; add the chicken, seasoned with 1/2 teaspoon of the salt. Turn to coat the thighs; reduce the heat to low and cook, covered, for 15 minutes. Remove the cover; cook for an additional 10 minutes, stirring occasionally. Remove the mixture to a bowl and cover with aluminum foil to keep warm.

Drain the rice. Wipe the pan clean; return to medium heat. Heat the remaining 2 tablespoons canola oil; add the sliced onion and sauté until lightly browned, about 5 minutes. Remove half the onion; set aside. Stir in the remaining 3/4 teaspoon salt, the remaining 1/2 teaspoon cumin, the cinnamon sticks, and cardamom. Stir in the rice; sauté for 1 minute. Stir the saffron in 2 cups boiling water to dissolve; add to the rice. Reduce the heat to low and cook, covered, for 12 minutes, or until the rice is tender and the liquid is absorbed. Layer the chicken mixture on top of the rice; cover and cook until heated through, 3 to 4 minutes. Sprinkle the raisins, cashews, reserved sliced onion, cilantro, and mint over the top.

MAKE AHEAD Cook the rice for 8 minutes or until a bit of liquid remains. Transfer to a 13 × 9-inch baking dish and let cool. Top with the chicken and refrigerate. When ready to serve, bake, covered with aluminum foil, in a 350°F oven for 30 to 40 minutes. Remove the foil and sprinkle with the cashews and other ingredients as indicated above.

SERVE WITH A cauliflower salad and a side dish of plain yogurt plus naan.

Occasionally, my good friend and fellow cookbook author Raghavan Iyer and I get together and cook. We combine our talents and culinary training, Raghavan's in Indian and mine in French, to come up with some spectacular combinations.

I've done a bit of that combining in this recipe, inspired by our cook-a-thons, taking northern Indian almond and saffron-based korma sauce and adding French crème fraîche. This addition enhances the almond flavor, adds extra body to the sauce, and keeps it from curdling.

Chicken Korma

MAKES 4 SERVINGS

❄

2 TABLESPOONS HOT MILK

1/2 TEASPOON CRUMBLED
SAFFRON THREADS

1/3 CUP CRÈME FRAÎCHE

3/4 TEASPOON SALT

1/2 TEASPOON CAYENNE

FOUR 6-OUNCE BONELESS,
SKINLESS CHICKEN BREAST
HALVES

2/3 CUP SLIVERED ALMONDS

1 TEASPOON GARAM MASALA

1/4 TEASPOON GROUND CUMIN

1/2 CUP REDUCED-SODIUM
CHICKEN BROTH

1 TABLESPOON CANOLA OIL

2 TABLESPOONS
CHOPPED GINGER

3 LARGE GARLIC CLOVES,
MINCED (ABOUT
1 1/2 TABLESPOONS)

3 LARGE ROMA TOMATOES,
CHOPPED (ABOUT 1 1/2 CUPS)

2 TABLESPOONS FRESH
CILANTRO LEAVES

Stir the milk and saffron together in a small bowl; let steep for about 5 minutes. Combine the crème fraîche, salt, and cayenne in a 1-gallon self-sealing plastic bag; pour in the saffron milk and squeeze to combine. Add the chicken; squeeze and turn to coat. Marinate for 45 minutes at room temperature.

Meanwhile, pulse the almonds in the bowl of a small food processor with the garam masala and cumin until finely ground; add the chicken broth and pulse to combine. (Or place the almonds, garam masala, cumin, and broth in a blender and grind together.)

Heat the canola oil in a large skillet over medium heat. Add the ginger and garlic; sauté until fragrant, 30 seconds to 1 minute. Add the chicken and marinade; cook the chicken on each side for 3 minutes. Add the tomatoes; reduce the heat to low. Cover and cook for 5 minutes. Add the ground almond mixture, stirring to combine. Turn the chicken; cover and cook until the chicken is no longer pink in the thickest portion when cut with a knife, 10 to 15 minutes. Serve garnished with the cilantro leaves. *(continued)*

MAKE AHEAD Marinate the chicken for up to 6 hours in the refrigerator. Prepare the ground almond mixture ahead and refrigerate. When ready, heat the oil in the skillet and proceed as directed.

SERVE WITH Basmati rice, naan, and green beans.

The word *rouladen* is German and is used to describe rolled meat combinations such as this one. Here, the filling is simple—just mustard, ham, and green onions—but there is nothing simple about the flavor. Spiked with tiny nonpareil capers in the creamy sauce, the outcome is truly *wunderbar*.

Chicken Rouladen

MAKES 4 SERVINGS

✳

FOUR 6-OUNCE BONELESS, SKINLESS CHICKEN BREAST HALVES

$1/4$ CUP DIJON MUSTARD

4 SLICES HAM

4 GREEN ONIONS, WHITE AND PALE GREEN PORTIONS, CHOPPED

$1/8$ TEASPOON SALT

$1/8$ TEASPOON FRESHLY GROUND PEPPER

1 TABLESPOON CANOLA OIL

1 TABLESPOON SALTED BUTTER

$3/4$ CUP REDUCED-SODIUM CHICKEN BROTH

$1/2$ CUP HEAVY CREAM

1 TABLESPOON NONPAREIL CAPERS (IN VINEGAR), RINSED

Flatten the chicken breasts to about $1/4$-inch thickness between two pieces of plastic wrap with a rolling pin. Spread each with 1 tablespoon mustard; top with a slice of ham. Scatter the chopped green onions over the ham. Season with salt and pepper. Roll each into a cylinder; fasten with kitchen twine or toothpicks into oval bundles.

Heat the canola oil and butter in a large skillet over medium-high heat. When sizzling, add the chicken and sauté until browned, 3 to 4 minutes per side.

Add the chicken broth; reduce the heat to low. Simmer, covered, until the chicken is no longer pink in the thickest portion when cut with a knife, about 10 minutes. Remove.

Add the cream and capers; increase the heat to high. Boil until reduced by half and slightly thickened, 3 to 4 minutes. Return the chicken to the skillet or arrange on a platter and pour the sauce over all.

MAKE AHEAD Have the chicken filled, rolled, and ready to cook up to several hours in advance. Complete the recipe when desired.

SERVE WITH Roasted potatoes, a tomato-topped salad, and crusty rolls.

More like a frittata than our Western expectations of a tagine, this combination of chicken and eggs makes a great brunch or light supper dish. I've taken the liberty of using cooked, diced chicken rather than the traditional chicken on the bone for ease of eating and as an excellent way to use up leftovers. Around Thanksgiving, try turkey instead. Cooking the eggs in a firmer than traditional style makes the tagine easier to serve.

MAKES 4 SERVINGS

❊

2 TABLESPOONS OLIVE OIL

1 SMALL ONION, CHOPPED
(ABOUT 1/2 CUP)

1 CUP COOKED, DICED CHICKEN

3/4 TEASPOON SALT

1/2 TEASPOON CINNAMON

1/4 TEASPOON GROUND CUMIN

PINCH CAYENNE

1 TABLESPOON LEMON JUICE

8 LARGE EGGS

1 TABLESPOON CHOPPED
FRESH PARSLEY

1/8 TEASPOON FRESHLY
GROUND PEPPER

Djaj Souiri

(Chicken and Egg Tagine)

Heat the olive oil in a 10-inch nonstick skillet over medium heat. Add the onion; sauté until softened, 4 to 5 minutes. Stir in the chicken, 1/2 teaspoon of the salt, the cinnamon, cumin, and cayenne. Reduce the heat to low; stir in 2 tablespoons water and the lemon juice; let simmer until the liquid has evaporated, about 2 minutes.

Meanwhile, beat the eggs with the parsley, the remaining 1/4 teaspoon salt, and the pepper in a medium bowl. Pour the egg mixture into the skillet; cook, covered, for 5 minutes. Push the sides with a fork, letting the uncooked egg run down toward the bottom of the pan. Cover and cook, occasionally cutting into the eggs with a spatula and tilting the pan to allow the uncooked eggs to run to the bottom, until just set, 5 to 7 additional minutes. Cut into fourths and serve.

MAKE AHEAD Sauté the onion and add the chicken. Refrigerate the mixture, covered, until ready to use. Reheat over low heat, stirring in the seasonings, then the water and lemon juice. Proceed as directed.

SERVE WITH Apricot muffins for a brunch plus a red onion and orange–topped tossed salad. For a light supper, substitute pita bread for the muffins.

7 Wok-Based Dishes

hat could be more Hawaiian than pineapple paired with tender pieces of chicken and topped with rich and crunchy macadamia nuts? The chicken stays moist by tossing it first in a mixture of soy and cornstarch, giving the exterior a velvety mouthfeel.

Hawaiian Pineapple Chicken

MAKES 4 SERVINGS

❊

THREE 5- TO 6-OUNCE
BONELESS, SKINLESS CHICKEN
BREAST HALVES, CUT IN 1-INCH
CUBES

2 TEASPOONS PLUS
3 TABLESPOONS SOY SAUCE

6 TEASPOONS CORNSTARCH

TWO 8-OUNCE CANS PINEAPPLE
CHUNKS IN JUICE

2 TABLESPOONS CHOPPED
GINGER

3/4 TEASPOON FIVE-SPICE
POWDER

1 LARGE GARLIC CLOVE,
CHOPPED (ABOUT
1 1/2 TEASPOONS)

3 TABLESPOONS CANOLA OIL

1 RED BELL PEPPER, CUT IN
3/4-INCH CUBES

1 GREEN BELL PEPPER, CUT IN
3/4-INCH CUBES

1/2 CUP COARSELY CHOPPED
MACADAMIA NUTS

Toss the chicken with the 2 teaspoons soy sauce in a medium bowl. Sprinkle with 1 teaspoon of the cornstarch and stir to coat. Set aside. Mix the remaining 3 tablespoons soy sauce and 5 teaspoons cornstarch in a small bowl. Drain the juice from the pineapple chunks into the soy-sauce-and-cornstarch mixture. Stir in 1 tablespoon of the ginger and the five-spice powder; set aside. Reserve the pineapple chunks. Blend the remaining 1 tablespoon ginger and the garlic in a small bowl; set aside.

Heat 2 tablespoons of the canola oil in a wok over high heat; swirl to coat the sides. Add half the ginger-garlic mixture; stir quickly. Add the chicken; stir-fry until the chicken is no longer pink in the center when cut with a knife, 4 to 5 minutes. Remove.

Add the remaining 1 tablespoon canola oil; swirl to coat the sides. Add the remaining ginger-garlic mixture; stir quickly. Add the red and green bell peppers; stir-fry for 2 minutes. Return the chicken to the wok; add the drained pineapple chunks. Quickly stir the soy-cornstarch mixture to blend and pour into the wok. Stir to coat the chicken and peppers; continue stirring until the liquid boils and thickens, 1 to 2 minutes. Sprinkle with the macadamia nuts and serve.

MAKE AHEAD Have all the ingredients prepped and organized ahead of time.

SERVE WITH An avocado and hearts of palm–topped green salad and jasmine rice.

Chinese black bean sauce adds a salty pungency to the chicken and sweet potatoes in this simply made stir-fry, establishing a ying and yang kind of contrast that works particularly well. These black beans are fermented, salted soybeans, quite different from those found in Southwestern or Latin American cooking. If you can't find black bean sauce, substitute brown bean sauce or yellow bean sauce.

Chicken with Black Bean Sauce

MAKES 4 SERVINGS

✳

1 LEMON

2 MEDIUM SWEET POTATOES OR
RED GARNET YAMS

$^1/_4$ CUP CHINESE
BLACK BEAN SAUCE

2 TABLESPOONS SHERRY

2 TEASPOONS SOY SAUCE

2 TEASPOONS SUGAR

$^1/_8$ TEASPOON GROUND
WHITE PEPPER

3 TABLESPOONS CANOLA OIL

2 LARGE GARLIC CLOVES,
MINCED (ABOUT 1 TABLESPOON)

1 TABLESPOON MINCED GINGER

THREE 6- TO 8-OUNCE
BONELESS, SKINLESS CHICKEN
BREAST HALVES, CUT IN
$^1/_8$-INCH STRIPS

1 LARGE RED ONION, CUT IN
HALF LENGTHWISE, THEN IN
$^1/_4$-INCH SLICES

2 TEASPOONS TOASTED
SESAME OIL

2 GREEN ONIONS, WHITE AND
TENDER GREEN PORTIONS,
THINLY SLICED

Juice the lemon and place 2 tablespoons of the juice in a small bowl. Pour the remaining juice in a medium bowl and half fill with cold water. Peel the sweet potatoes and halve lengthwise; slice into $^1/_4$-inch half-moons and place in the bowl with the lemon water to prevent browning. Set aside. Add the black bean sauce, sherry, soy sauce, sugar, and white pepper to the 2 tablespoons lemon juice and stir to combine. Set aside.

Heat 2 tablespoons of the canola oil in a wok over high heat; swirl to coat the sides. Add half the garlic and half the ginger to the pan; stir quickly. Add the chicken. Stir-fry until the chicken is no longer pink in the center when cut with a knife, 3 to 4 minutes; remove. Take the wok briefly from the heat.

Drain the sweet potato slices, patting them dry with a paper towel. Return the wok to high heat. Add the remaining 1 tablespoon canola oil to the wok; swirl to coat the sides. Add the remaining garlic and ginger, stir quickly. Add the sweet potatoes; stir-fry for 1 minute. Add the onion; stir-fry for 1 minute. Add $^1/_2$ cup water; cover and cook until the potatoes are tender when pierced with a knife, about 3 minutes. Remove the cover and add the black bean mixture. Stir in the chicken and cook briefly to reheat, about 1 minute. Stir in the sesame oil. Remove from the heat; sprinkle with the green onions and serve.

MAKE AHEAD Have all the ingredients organized, sliced, and assembled ahead of time, then stir-fry when ready.

SERVE WITH A side dish of rice.

Oyster sauce is a commonly used condiment in Chinese cooking. While it contains oysters, the finished product has no fishy taste. It is readily available in the Asian section of most grocery stores. My preference, however, is to shop, whenever possible, at an Asian market, where the ingredients are far more authentic and of better quality.

Chicken with Broccoli and Oyster Sauce

MAKES 4 SERVINGS

✳

$1/3$ CUP OYSTER SAUCE

2 TABLESPOONS SOY SAUCE

2 TABLESPOONS RICE WINE (OR SHERRY)

1 TEASPOON TOASTED SESAME OIL

THREE 6-OUNCE BONELESS, SKINLESS CHICKEN BREAST HALVES, CUT IN 3 × $1/4$-INCH STRIPS

1 POUND BROCCOLI, THE STEMS PEELED AND CUT IN $1/4$-INCH SLICES AND THE CROWN BROKEN INTO FLORETS

1 TABLESPOON CANOLA OR PEANUT OIL

1 TABLESPOON MINCED GINGER

2 LARGE GARLIC CLOVES, MINCED (ABOUT 1 TABLESPOON)

10 GREEN ONIONS, WHITE AND TENDER GREEN PORTIONS, CUT IN HALF LENGTHWISE, THEN IN 1-INCH PIECES

2 TEASPOONS CORNSTARCH

$1/2$ CUP WALNUTS

Combine the oyster sauce, 1 tablespoon of the soy sauce, 1 tablespoon of the rice wine, and the sesame oil in a small bowl; set aside. Combine the chicken, the remaining 1 tablespoon soy sauce, and the remaining 1 tablespoon rice wine in a medium bowl; stir well to coat. Set aside.

Pour $2/3$ cup water into a wok; heat over medium-high heat. When simmering, add the sliced broccoli and cover; steam for 2 minutes. Add the broccoli florets and cover; steam until crisp-tender, an additional 3 to 4 minutes. Remove and drain.

Heat the canola oil in the wok over high heat; swirl to coat the sides. Add the ginger and garlic. Stir quickly; add the chicken. Stir-fry until the chicken is no longer pink when cut with a knife, 3 to 4 minutes. Add the broccoli and the oyster sauce mixture; bring to a boil. Stir in the green onions. Dissolve the cornstarch in 2 tablespoons water in a small bowl; add to the wok and stir to combine. Cook until thickened, about 1 minute. Stir in the walnuts; serve.

MAKE AHEAD Have everything organized and ready to stir-fry.

SERVE WITH Jasmine rice.

Chicken with cashews, found in both the Hunan and Szechwan provinces of China, normally includes bell pepper and onion. Another popular Chinese offering is stir-fried green beans flavored with hoisin sauce. I've done a bit of fusion cooking here by combining the two recipes, yet staying within the same country. Adding the beans to the chicken works very well and makes for a complete main course in one wok.

Feel free to make this dish as spicy as you like by varying the amount of chile paste with garlic.

Chicken with Cashews

Toss the chicken with 1 tablespoon of the soy sauce and the rice wine in a medium bowl. Sprinkle with the cornstarch; stir to coat. Mix together the remaining 1 tablespoon soy sauce and the hoisin sauce; set aside.

Heat 1 tablespoon of the peanut oil in a wok over high heat; swirl to coat the sides. Add half the ginger and half the chile paste; stir quickly. Add the chicken; stir-fry until the chicken is no longer pink when cut with a knife, 3 to 5 minutes. Remove.

Add the remaining 2 tablespoons peanut oil to the wok; swirl to coat the sides. Add the remaining ginger and chile paste; stir quickly. Add the bell pepper, onion, and mushrooms. Stir-fry for 2 minutes; add the green beans. Continue to stir-fry until the beans turn bright green, 1 to 2 minutes. Add $^1/_2$ cup water; continue to stir-fry until the vegetables are barely cooked through, 4 to 5 minutes. Return the chicken to the wok; stir in the hoisin mixture. Cook until the chicken is heated through, about 1 minute. Sprinkle with the cashews; serve immediately. *(continued)*

MAKE AHEAD The key to quickly made stir-fries is to prep everything ahead. Have all the vegetables cut and in small bowls. Cut the chicken into strips ahead of time. Refrigerate everything, covered, until ready to stir-fry. Proceed with the recipe and your meal will be ready in minutes.

SERVE WITH Rice, as always, to complete stir-fried meals. For a cooling accompaniment, marinate thinly sliced cucumber in $^1/_4$ cup rice vinegar, 3 to 4 teaspoons soy sauce, and $^1/_2$ teaspoon toasted sesame oil.

Kung pao chicken, from the Chinese province of Szechwan, is characteristically spicy and always contains peanuts. The peanuts also determine the shape of the remaining ingredients, with everything cut in small squares to mimic the nut's silhouette.

Kung Pao Chicken

MAKES 4 SERVINGS

✳

1½ POUNDS BONELESS, SKINLESS CHICKEN BREASTS, CUT IN ¾-INCH CUBES

2 TABLESPOONS SOY SAUCE

1 TABLESPOON SHERRY

1 TABLESPOON PLUS 1 TEASPOON CORNSTARCH

¼ CUP REDUCED-SODIUM CHICKEN BROTH (OR WATER)

1 TABLESPOON HOISIN SAUCE

1 TEASPOON SUGAR

½ TEASPOON SESAME OIL

3 TABLESPOONS PEANUT OR CANOLA OIL

½ CUP RAW PEANUTS

1½ TEASPOONS MINCED GARLIC

1½ TEASPOONS MINCED GINGER

1 TO 2 TEASPOONS CHINESE OR VIETNAMESE CHILE PASTE OR SAUCE WITH GARLIC

1 RED BELL PEPPER, CUT IN ¾-INCH CUBES

1 GREEN BELL PEPPER, CUT IN ¾-INCH CUBES

8 GREEN ONIONS, WHITE AND PALE GREEN PORTIONS, CUT IN HALF LENGTHWISE, THEN IN ¾-INCH PIECES

Place the chicken in a medium bowl; drizzle with 1 tablespoon of the soy sauce and the sherry. Sprinkle with the 1 tablespoon cornstarch and mix to coat. Marinate for 15 minutes.

Stir together the chicken broth, hoisin sauce, remaining 1 tablespoon soy sauce, remaining 1 teaspoon cornstarch, the sugar, and sesame oil in a small bowl. Set aside.

Heat 2 tablespoons of the peanut oil in a wok over high heat; swirl to coat the sides. Add the peanuts; stir-fry until pale brown, 2 to 3 minutes. Remove with a slotted spoon.

Add the garlic, ginger, and chile paste; stir quickly. Add the chicken; stir-fry until the chicken is no longer pink in the center when cut with a knife, 4 to 5 minutes. Remove to a separate plate.

Add the remaining 1 tablespoon peanut oil; add the bell peppers and green onions. Stir-fry until crisp-tender, about 2 minutes. Return the chicken to the wok; stir the cornstarch mixture to blend. Add to the wok. Stir to combine and boil until thickened, about 1 minute. Toss with the peanuts; serve.

MAKE AHEAD Prepare and assemble everything in advance of cooking.

SERVE WITH Lots of rice to offset the heat plus steamed broccoli.

*L*emon chicken most often appears as pieces of chicken battered, deep-fried, and topped with a thick, lemony sauce. While tasty, it's tricky for the home cook to get just right, plus the dish is laden with calories. By stir-frying strips of chicken and adding asparagus, then adding the lemon sauce toward the end of cooking, this recipe becomes a true one-pot—or one-wok—dish.

Lemon Chicken Stir-Fry

MAKES 4 SERVINGS

❈

¹/4 CUP LEMON JUICE

2 TABLESPOONS HONEY

¹/2 TEASPOON GRATED
LEMON ZEST

¹/2 TEASPOON PLUS
2 TEASPOONS MINCED GARLIC

¹/4 TEASPOON SALT

¹/4 TEASPOON GRATED
GINGER, PLUS 2 TEASPOONS
MINCED GINGER

¹/3 CUP REDUCED-SODIUM
CHICKEN BROTH

2 TEASPOONS CORNSTARCH

3 TABLESPOONS CANOLA OIL

THREE 6- TO 8-OUNCE
BONELESS, SKINLESS CHICKEN
BREAST HALVES, CUT IN
¹/4-INCH STRIPS

¹/2 POUND THIN ASPARAGUS
SPEARS, TRIMMED AND CUT IN
2-INCH LENGTHS

2 LARGE CARROTS, PEELED
AND CUT IN 2 × ¹/4-INCH
STRIPS

1 SMALL RED ONION, HALVED
LENGTHWISE AND CUT IN
¹/4-INCH SLICES

Stir the lemon juice and honey together in a small bowl to dissolve the honey; stir in the lemon zest. Mash the ¹/2 teaspoon minced garlic with the salt using the back of the tines of a fork to form a paste; stir the paste into the lemon mixture along with the grated ginger. Stir the chicken broth and cornstarch together in a separate small bowl.

Heat 2 tablespoons of the canola oil in a wok over high heat; swirl to coat the sides. Add 1 teaspoon of the remaining garlic and 1 teaspoon of the minced ginger to the wok and stir quickly. Add the chicken; stir-fry until the chicken is no longer pink in the center when cut with a knife, 3 to 4 minutes. Remove.

Add the remaining 1 tablespoon canola oil to the wok; swirl to coat the sides. Add the remaining 1 teaspoon garlic and the remaining 1 teaspoon minced ginger; stir quickly. Add the asparagus, carrots, and onion; stir-fry for 2 minutes. Add the lemon mixture and bring to a boil. Boil, stirring often, until the vegetables are crisp-tender, 2 to 3 minutes.

Add the reserved chicken. Stir the cornstarch mixture to blend; pour into the wok. Bring to a boil; boil until thickened and clear, about 1 minute.

MAKE AHEAD Have everything prepped and assembled in advance.

SERVE WITH Rice to soak up the lemon sauce.

$\mathcal{I}$'m not a huge fan of preparing the traditional sweet-and-sour chicken offered in Chinese restaurants. I think it's the coating that stops me from making it at home; it's hard to get it as crisp as it should be. Yet the idea of sweet and sour is an appealing one. While traveling through China on a cultural tour, our group was often served chicken that was battered and then covered with a sweet-and-sour glaze. This familiar item, sometimes surrounded by unrecognizable offerings, was a sure hit. What I've done to solve the problem of a crispy batter is to eliminate it, leaving the chicken simply coated with the sauce after stir-frying with sweet bell peppers.

Sweet-and-Sour Chicken Stir-Fry

MAKES 4 SERVINGS

✵

6 TABLESPOONS RICE VINEGAR

$^1/_4$ CUP SUGAR

$^1/_4$ CUP SOY SAUCE

2 LARGE GARLIC CLOVES, CHOPPED (ABOUT 1 TABLESPOON), PLUS 1 MEDIUM GARLIC CLOVE, MINCED (ABOUT $^3/_4$ TEASPOON)

$^1/_2$ TEASPOON SALT

6 TABLESPOONS KETCHUP

2 TEASPOONS FINELY GRATED ORANGE ZEST

1 TEASPOON GRATED GINGER, PLUS $1^1/_2$ TEASPOONS MINCED GINGER

1 TEASPOON CHINESE OR VIETNAMESE CHILE PASTE OR SAUCE WITH GARLIC

$^1/_2$ CUP REDUCED-SODIUM CHICKEN BROTH

Stir the rice vinegar, sugar, and soy sauce together in a medium bowl until the sugar is dissolved. Mash the chopped garlic with the salt, using the back of the tines of a fork to form a paste, and stir the paste into the vinegar mixture. Stir in the ketchup until well blended. Stir in the orange zest, grated ginger, and chile paste. Set aside. Stir the chicken broth and cornstarch together in a small bowl to dissolve. Stir in the sesame oil. Set aside.

Heat 2 tablespoons of the canola oil in a wok over high heat; swirl to coat the sides. Add the minced garlic and minced ginger; stir quickly. Add the chicken; stir-fry until no longer pink in the center when cut with a knife, 4 to 5 minutes. Remove.

Add the remaining 1 tablespoon canola oil to the wok; swirl to coat the sides. Add the bell peppers and onion; stir-fry for 2 minutes. Add the vinegar mixture and bring to a boil; boil for 30 seconds. Stir the cornstarch mixture to blend and add to the wok. Stir to combine; bring to a boil and boil until the liquid is thickened and clear, about 1 minute. Stir in the chicken and cook briefly to reheat, about 1 minute.

MAKE AHEAD Have everything prepped and assembled in advance.

SERVE WITH Bowls of medium-grain rice, cooked to a slightly sticky consistency so the grains hold together when eaten with chopsticks.

1 TABLESPOON CORNSTARCH

1 TEASPOON TOASTED SESAME OIL

3 TABLESPOONS CANOLA OIL

THREE 6- TO 8-OUNCE BONELESS, SKINLESS CHICKEN BREAST HALVES, CUT IN 1-INCH CUBES

1 RED BELL PEPPER, CUT IN 3/4-INCH CUBES

1 GREEN BELL PEPPER, CUT IN 3/4-INCH CUBES

1 SMALL RED ONION, CUT IN 3/4-INCH WEDGES

$\mathcal{I}$n China a wok is a truly versatile cooking utensil, used to stir-fry, but also to steam, braise, and even smoke. Its curved shape is meant to capture every last kilocalorie of valuable heat, and its generous capacity will accommodate the whole small chicken and the steamer basket called for here.

While this dish traditionally uses Szechwan peppercorns, they have been banned in this country recently for agricultural reasons. I've made a few modifications to compensate, but kept the essence of the recipe intact.

Tea-Smoked Chicken

MAKES 4 SERVINGS

☀

1¹/₂ TEASPOONS BLACK PEPPERCORNS

1¹/₂ TEASPOONS SZECHWAN SEASONING MIX, SUCH AS SCHILLING

1¹/₄ TEASPOONS SALT

ONE 2¹/₂- TO 3-POUND CHICKEN

2 GINGER SLICES

¹/₃ CUP LAPSANG SOUCHONG OR REGULAR BLACK TEA

3 TABLESPOONS RICE

2 TABLESPOONS PACKED LIGHT BROWN SUGAR

1 TEASPOON FIVE-SPICE POWDER

1 CINNAMON STICK

1¹/₂ TEASPOONS TOASTED SESAME OIL

Place the peppercorns in a wok over medium heat. Toast the peppercorns until fragrant, shaking occasionally, 4 to 5 minutes. Remove and let cool slightly. Crush or grind coarsely; mix with the Szechwan seasoning and salt in a small bowl. Pat the chicken dry and season inside and out with the peppercorn mixture. Place the ginger in the cavity.

Place a collapsible steamer basket in the bottom of a wok. Add enough water to the bottom of the wok to reach about ¹/₂ inch below the basket. Place the chicken in the basket. Heat the wok over medium heat until the water boils. Reduce the heat to medium-low; cover and steam the chicken until a thermometer reaches 180°F when inserted in the thickest portion of the thigh, 40 to 45 minutes. (Check occasionally and add hot water as needed to prevent the wok from going dry.) Remove the chicken in its steamer basket; drain off the water.

Meanwhile, combine the tea, rice, brown sugar, and five-spice powder in a small bowl. Once the chicken is steamed, let the wok cool for several minutes. When it is cool enough to handle, clean and wipe dry; line the wok and the lid with aluminum foil. Add the tea mixture and cinnamon stick to the bottom of the foil-lined wok; top with the chicken in the steamer basket. Cover and heat over medium heat. When wisps of smoke emerge, about 5 minutes, begin timing and smoke the chicken for 15 minutes. Remove the wok from the heat and, without removing the cover, let the chicken rest in the wok for 20 minutes. Remove the chicken; discard the ginger slices and drizzle with the sesame oil. Cut into pieces and serve.

MAKE AHEAD Complete the recipe up to drizzling with sesame oil. Refrigerate, covered. When ready, reheat in a 350°F oven for 20 to 30 minutes.

SERVE WITH Rice plus a cold, mixed vegetable salad dressed with rice wine and topped with almonds to fill out the menu.

Thailand uses several curry pastes, each mixed with particular ingredients to form a complete dish. One combination is green curry paste with chicken and eggplant. Thai eggplants are small and round; they can be difficult to find. I've substituted the thin, violet-hued Japanese eggplant which is easier to locate and works well. Even the more substantial, classic, deep purple variety would be fine.

Green curry paste can be found in Asian markets or even in well-stocked supermarkets under the nationally distributed Taste of Thai label. As with all spicy foods, the amount of heat is adjustable. Feel free to use more or less green curry paste depending on your personal preference.

Green Curry with Eggplant

MAKES 4 SERVINGS

❋

ONE 14-OUNCE CAN
COCONUT MILK

2 TABLESPOONS GREEN CURRY
PASTE

1$^{1}/_{2}$ POUNDS JAPANESE
EGGPLANT, CUT IN SCANT
$^{1}/_{2}$-INCH SLICES
(ABOUT 6 CUPS)

1 TEASPOON GRATED
LEMON ZEST

THREE 5- TO 6-OUNCE
BONELESS, SKINLESS
CHICKEN BREAST HALVES, CUT
IN 1-INCH CUBES

$^{1}/_{4}$ CUP FRESH BASIL LEAVES

1 SERRANO CHILE, CUT IN VERY
THIN SLIVERS

Bring $^{1}/_{2}$ cup of the coconut milk to a boil in a wok over medium-high heat; boil until thickened, 4 to 5 minutes. Stir in the green curry paste. Add the eggplant slices and toss to coat. Stir in the remaining coconut milk and the lemon zest; reduce the heat to medium-low and cook for 5 minutes.

Add the chicken; cook, stirring occasionally, adding small amounts of water as necessary if the sauce thickens too much, until the chicken is no longer pink in the center when cut with a knife, about 10 minutes. Stir in 2 tablespoons of the basil leaves; garnish with the remaining basil leaves and the slivered serrano.

MAKE AHEAD Have all the ingredients prepped and organized ahead of time.

SERVE WITH Jasmine rice. As is the case with so many spicy dishes, a cooling cucumber salad is the perfect foil.

*A*long with green—and red—curry paste, Thai cooks use a yellow paste, traditionally added to either a chicken or shrimp and potato curry. Look for this paste in Asian grocery stores or online.

I've added green beans to make the one-pot concept more complete; sugar snap peas work as well, but add them during the last 5 minutes of cooking.

Yellow Curry with Potatoes

MAKES 4 SERVINGS

❄

1 TABLESPOON CANOLA OIL

2 TEASPOONS CHOPPED GINGER

1 TABLESPOON
YELLOW CURRY PASTE

ONE 14-OUNCE CAN
COCONUT MILK

2 TABLESPOONS NAM PLA
(FISH SAUCE)

1 TABLESPOON PACKED LIGHT
BROWN SUGAR

8 FINGERLING POTATOES
(ABOUT 3/4 POUND), PEELED
AND CUT IN 1/2-INCH SLICES

1 CUP FROZEN PEARL ONIONS,
THAWED

THREE 5- TO 6-OUNCE
BONELESS, SKINLESS
CHICKEN BREAST HALVES, CUT
IN 1-INCH CUBES

1 CUP GREEN BEANS CUT IN
1 1/2-INCH LENGTHS

Heat the canola oil in a wok over high heat; swirl to coat the sides. Add the ginger; stir quickly and then stir in the curry paste. Add the coconut milk and stir to blend. Stir in the nam pla and brown sugar; add the potatoes and pearl onions. Reduce the heat to medium-low and gently boil for 10 minutes, stirring occasionally. Add the chicken and green beans, thinning the sauce as necessary with a bit of water; cook until the chicken is no longer pink in the center when cut with a knife, the potatoes are tender, and the green beans are crisp-tender, about 10 minutes.

MAKE AHEAD Have all the ingredients prepped, measured, and ready to cook ahead of time. The dish itself comes together in less than a half hour.

SERVE WITH While this dish is traditionally served with jasmine rice, the potatoes may make the rice seem redundant. I like to serve a simple lettuce salad sprinkled with cilantro and mint as an accompaniment.

*L*emongrass is very common in Vietnamese recipes. Its outer leaves are tough and should be discarded, as should any woody portions of its bulbous base. The easiest way to chop lemongrass is in the bowl of a mini-food processor. Cut the stalk into ½-inch pieces and place in the bowl of the processor fitted with the metal blade. Pulse to process to the desired consistency.

Vietnamese Lemongrass Chicken

MAKES 4 SERVINGS

2 LEMONGRASS STALKS,
TENDER PORTIONS ONLY,
FINELY CHOPPED

1 TEASPOON GRATED LIME ZEST

2 TABLESPOONS LIME JUICE

1 TABLESPOON NUOC MAM
(FISH SAUCE)

1¼ POUNDS BONELESS,
SKINLESS CHICKEN BREAST
STRIPS (OR HALVES, CUT IN
THIN STRIPS)

2 TABLESPOONS CANOLA OIL

1 TABLESPOON MINCED GINGER

2 LARGE GARLIC CLOVES,
CHOPPED (ABOUT
1 TABLESPOON)

1 TEASPOON CHINESE OR
VIETNAMESE CHILE PASTE OR
SAUCE WITH GARLIC

4 LARGE SHALLOTS, SLICED
(ABOUT 1 CUP)

Combine the lemongrass, lime zest, lime juice, and nuoc mam in a 1-gallon self-sealing plastic bag; squeeze to blend. Add the chicken; turn and squeeze to coat. Marinate for 30 minutes at room temperature.

Heat the canola oil in a wok over high heat; swirl to coat the sides. Add the ginger, garlic, and chile paste; stir quickly. Add the chicken with the marinade; stir-fry for 2 minutes. Add the shallots; continue to stir-fry until the chicken is no longer pink in the center when cut with a knife, an additional 4 to 5 minutes.

MAKE AHEAD Because of the high acidity of the marinade, I don't like to let the chicken marinate too long before cooking. Have the marinade ready and in the self-sealing bag. If necessary, the time period for marinating the chicken can be extended up to 1 hour, refrigerated. When ready, stir-fry as directed.

SERVE WITH Jasmine rice and a lettuce, cucumber, and tomato salad mixed with basil leaves and tossed with a lime juice and oil vinaigrette for a simple but tasty meal.

I've taken the wok-cooked Vietnamese Lemongrass Chicken and turned it into another one-dish offering. This time the dish is a salad bowl, and there's no extra cooking involved, only some assembly required.

Vietnamese Lemongrass Chicken Salad

MAKES 4 SERVINGS

✳

1 TABLESPOON RICE VINEGAR

2 TEASPOONS NUOC MAM
(FISH SAUCE)

1/2 TEASPOON SUGAR

2 TABLESPOONS CANOLA OIL

6 CUPS ROMAINE OR
LEAF LETTUCE

1/4 CUP TORN FRESH
MINT LEAVES

1/4 CUP CILANTRO LEAVES

1/2 CUP LIGHTLY BLANCHED
SUGAR SNAP PEAS, CUT ON THE
DIAGONAL IN 1/2-INCH PIECES

1 LARGE CARROT, PEELED AND
CUT IN 2 × 1/4-INCH STRIPS
(ABOUT 1 CUP)

1 RECIPE VIETNAMESE
LEMONGRASS CHICKEN
(PAGE 172), HOT OR COLD

Stir the rice vinegar, nuoc mam, and sugar together in a small bowl until the sugar is dissolved. Stir in the canola oil to make a dressing.

Toss the romaine, mint, and cilantro together in a large bowl. Scatter the sugar snap peas and carrot over the greens. Top with the Vietnamese Lemongrass Chicken. Stir the dressing again to combine and drizzle over the salad.

MAKE AHEAD Have the chicken cooked and all the salad ingredients ready to combine. Assemble right before serving.

SERVE WITH This is truly a meal in a bowl, but add a bit of French bread, if desired.

8 Specialty Cooking

Here, the chicken's pot is a packet, and each person gets his or her own. Taken from a classic method for campfire cooking, this muss-free aluminum foil—wrapped meal is great for a quickly prepared dinner on the grill at home or on vacation.

Hobo Chicken Foil Packets

MAKES 4 SERVINGS

✳

2 MEDIUM YUKON GOLD POTATOES (ABOUT 1 POUND), PEELED AND CUT IN $^1/_4$-INCH SLICES

$^1/_4$ TEASPOON SALT

$^1/_4$ TEASPOON FRESHLY GROUND PEPPER

FOUR 6 TO 8-OUNCE BONELESS, SKINLESS CHICKEN BREAST HALVES

1 SMALL ZUCCHINI, CUT IN $^1/_4$-INCH SLICES

1 SMALL YELLOW SQUASH, CUT IN $^1/_4$-INCH SLICES

FOUR $^1/_4$-INCH SLICES ONION

FOUR $^1/_4$-INCH RINGS RED BELL PEPPER

ONE 14$^1/_2$-OUNCE CAN DICED TOMATOES IN JUICE WITH BASIL, GARLIC, AND OREGANO

$^1/_2$ CUP FRESHLY GRATED PARMIGIANO-REGGIANO

Heat the grill to medium-high heat. Spray four 18 × 12-inch sheets of aluminum foil with nonstick spray.

Divide the potatoes among the foil sheets, arranging them in a single layer in the center of each sheet; season with the salt and $^1/_8$ teaspoon of the pepper. Top the potatoes with the chicken; scatter the zucchini and yellow squash slices over the chicken. Top each with a slice of onion, separated into rings, and a ring of bell pepper. Divide the tomatoes and their juice evenly over all and season with the remaining $^1/_8$ teaspoon pepper. Bring up the two longer sides of the foil and fold twice, then fold the ends twice to seal, forming packets. Grill over direct heat for 11 to 13 minutes, or until the chicken is no longer pink in the center when cut with a knife. (To test for doneness, carefully open the top of one of the packets, allowing the steam to escape. If the chicken is not done, reclose and return briefly to the grill.) Serve with the grated Parmesan on the side.

MAKE AHEAD Have the packets done up and waiting in the refrigerator.

SERVE WITH Garlic bread, heated and wrapped in foil in the spirit of campfire cooking.

*L*ike the recipe for Hobo Chicken on page 175, each chicken breast is encased in its own individual packet. This time, the far more elegant medium of parchment paper serves as the cooking container. Topped with dollops of mustard-laced crème fraîche and asparagus spears, the chicken emerges from its wrapping perfectly moist and tender.

Chicken Breasts en Papillote

MAKES 4 SERVINGS

❄

FOUR 6-OUNCE BONELESS, SKINLESS CHICKEN BREAST HALVES

1/2 TEASPOON SALT

1/4 TEASPOON FRESHLY GROUND PEPPER

16 THIN ASPARAGUS SPEARS, TRIMMED AND CUT IN 2-INCH LENGTHS

1 LARGE CARROT, PEELED AND CUT IN 2 × 1/4-INCH STRIPS (ABOUT 1 CUP)

1 CUP 2 × 1/4-INCH LEEK STRIPS, WHITE PORTION ONLY

1/4 CUP TARRAGON DIJON MUSTARD

1/4 CUP CRÈME FRAÎCHE

2 TABLESPOONS WHITE WINE

Heat the oven to 400°F. Using four 15 × 12-inch sheets of parchment paper, fold each sheet in half to form a 12 × 7 1/2-inch rectangle. With the folded edge as the center, cut half of a heart, then open it up to form a whole heart shape. Lay each chicken breast, seasoned with some of the salt and pepper, lengthwise on one half of each heart. Top each with asparagus, carrot, and leek.

Blend the Dijon mustard, crème fraîche, and white wine together in a small bowl; spoon evenly over the breasts. Fold the empty side of each heart over the chicken. Making tiny pleats along the cut edges, seal the two halves together. Arrange on a baking sheet and bake for 20 minutes. Cut slits in the parchment and serve.

MAKE AHEAD Have the chicken assembled and wrapped in parchment up to several hours ahead. Refrigerate until ready to bake, then proceed as directed.

SERVE WITH Basmati rice and a walnut-topped tossed salad.

While fajitas typically call for grilling seasoned strips of meat, I like to leave my chicken breasts whole while cooking. They stay moist and are easier to turn. Here, the only cooking container needed is the handy broiler pan furnished with every oven. I turn to my broiler in the cold winter months instead of the outdoor grill, but either method works well.

I use larger, burrito-style flour tortillas when serving fajitas. They can be generously filled and wrapped and still hold everything without the filling falling out.

Broiler Chicken Fajitas

MAKES 4 SERVINGS

❋

1/4 CUP LIME JUICE

3 TABLESPOONS OLIVE OIL

3/4 TEASPOON GARLIC SALT

3/4 TEASPOON GROUND CUMIN

1/2 TEASPOON CHILI POWDER

1/4 TEASPOON DRIED OREGANO,
PREFERABLY MEXICAN

PINCH CAYENNE

THREE 6-OUNCE BONELESS,
SKINLESS CHICKEN BREAST
HALVES

1 RED BELL PEPPER, CUT IN
1/2-INCH STRIPS

1 GREEN BELL PEPPER,
CUT IN 1/2-INCH STRIPS

1 MEDIUM ONION, CUT IN
3/4-INCH WEDGES

4 LARGE (BURRITO-SIZED)
FLOUR TORTILLAS

SALSA

SOUR CREAM

GUACAMOLE

Combine the lime juice, 2 tablespoons of the olive oil, the garlic salt, cumin, chili powder, oregano, and cayenne in a 1-gallon self-sealing plastic bag; squeeze to blend. Add the chicken; seal and turn to coat. Marinate at room temperature for 45 minutes.

Meanwhile, heat the broiler, positioning the top rack 4 to 6 inches from the heat source. Toss the bell peppers and onion with the remaining 1 tablespoon olive oil. Wrap the tortillas in aluminum foil.

Place the marinated chicken on one side of the broiler pan; broil for 5 minutes. Remove and turn. Scatter the bell peppers and onion over the remaining surface of the broiler pan.

Place the foil-wrapped tortillas on a lower shelf in the oven and return the broiler pan to the top rack. Broil the chicken until it is no longer pink in the thickest portion when cut with a knife, about an additional 4 minutes.

Remove the tortillas from the oven and serve wrapped in foil to keep warm. Remove the vegetables to a serving bowl.

(continued)

Cut the chicken in thin strips and place in a separate serving bowl.

Each diner fills a warm tortilla with chicken strips and vegetables; tops the mixture with salsa, sour cream, and guacamole; and wraps the tortilla around everything for eating out of hand.

MAKE AHEAD To move dinner preparation along in a timely manner, slice the vegetables while the chicken is marinating. For entertaining, the chicken can marinate in the refrigerator for several hours and the vegetables can be presliced.

SERVE WITH A lovely green salad scattered with red onions and sliced oranges plus icy margaritas, beer, or limeade.

Traditionally wrapped in banana leaves and cooked in a *pib*—or pit—this Yucatán chicken dish adapts well to clay cookers. The moist clay envelops the chicken, substituting for the banana leaves, and the high oven heat duplicates the intensity of a fiery pit. Make sure to follow the manufacturer's directions when working with your clay cooker.

Pollo Pibil

MAKES 4 SERVINGS

✳

1¹/₂ TEASPOONS ANNATTO (ACHIOTE) SEEDS

¹/₂ TEASPOON BLACK PEPPERCORNS

¹/₂ TEASPOON CUMIN SEEDS

2 CLOVES

1¹/₂ TEASPOONS SALT

¹/₄ TEASPOON CINNAMON

²/₃ CUP ORANGE JUICE

¹/₄ CUP LIME JUICE

2 TABLESPOONS LEMON JUICE

2 LARGE GARLIC CLOVES, MINCED (ABOUT 1 TABLESPOON)

ONE 3¹/₂- TO 4-POUND CHICKEN, CUT IN PIECES

Grind the annatto seeds, peppercorns, cumin seeds, and cloves in a spice mill or a clean coffee grinder. Add the ground spices along with the salt and cinnamon to a 1-gallon self-sealing plastic bag. Add the orange, lime, and lemon juices along with the garlic and squeeze to combine. Add the chicken; seal and turn several times to coat. Marinate in the refrigerator for 1¹/₂ hours, turning several times while marinating.

Meanwhile, soak (if required) a clay cooker according to the manufacturer's directions. Arrange the chicken in the bottom of the cooker and pour in the marinade. Cover with the top of the cooker and place in a cold oven. Set the temperature for 450°F and roast for 1¹/₄ to 1¹/₂ hours, or until the chicken is no longer pink in the thickest portion when cut with a knife. Remove the chicken and skim the excess fat from the cooking juices. Return the chicken to the cooker and serve.

MAKE AHEAD Have the marinade ingredients ready in the plastic bag; add the chicken 1¹/₂ hours before baking.

SERVE WITH Warm tortillas and a jicama, avocado, and tomato–topped green salad.

The chicken is cooked in an all-American oven bag enhanced by a Cuban marinade, blending food cultures in a unique way. Look for mojo criollo marinade in the Latin American section of your supermarket.

Chicken in a Bag with Mojo Criollo Marinade

MAKES 4 SERVINGS

❈

ONE 3½ TO 4-POUND CHICKEN

1 CUP MOJO CRIOLLO MARINADE
(FROM A 24-OUNCE BOTTLE)

1 TABLESPOON ALL-PURPOSE
FLOUR

1 MEDIUM ONION, SLICED

½ TEASPOON DRIED THYME

½ TEASPOON GROUND CUMIN

¼ TEASPOON SALT

¼ TEASPOON FRESHLY GROUND
PEPPER

PINCH CAYENNE

½ ORANGE

2 CUPS BABY CARROTS

Place the chicken and marinade in a 1-gallon self-sealing plastic bag; turn to coat. Marinate in the refrigerator for 1½ hours, turning occasionally. Remove the chicken from the bag and discard the marinade.

Meanwhile, heat the oven to 350°F. Add the flour to a large oven bag; shake to coat the inside of the bag. Place the bag in a 13 × 9-inch baking pan, arranging the opening along the wide side of the pan. Place the sliced onion on the bottom of the bag.

Combine the thyme, cumin, salt, pepper, and cayenne in a small bowl. Sprinkle the exterior and interior of the chicken with the seasonings. Place the orange half inside the cavity and place the chicken in the prepared bag. Scatter the carrots around the chicken. Seal the bag with the provided tie; cut six ½-inch slits in the top of the bag.

Roast the chicken for 1 to 1¼ hours, or until a thermometer registers 180°F when inserted in the thickest portion of the thigh. (Puncture a hole in the bag with the thermometer to get a reading.)

Remove the chicken and carrots to a platter; using a double thickness of paper towels or a clean cloth to handle the hot orange half, squeeze the juice over the top of the chicken. Pour the roasting juices into a pitcher and serve separately.

MAKE AHEAD This is so easy that the only thing possible to do ahead is to marinate the chicken. Drain off the marinade and refrigerate the chicken in the same self-sealing bag until it's time to roast.

SERVE WITH Rice and a jicama and radish–topped green salad.

While recipes for chicken in the slow cooker abound, some are far superior to others. Extended cooking can cause chicken to fall apart. By capitalizing on this tendency and combining moist chicken thighs with a tangy-spicy barbecue sauce sparked with chipotle chile powder, this feed-a-crowd winner will have everyone asking for the recipe.

Slow-Cooked Pulled Barbecue Chicken

MAKES 12 SERVINGS

1 SMALL ONION, CHOPPED
(ABOUT ¹/₂ CUP)

1 LARGE GARLIC CLOVE, MINCED
(ABOUT 1¹/₂ TEASPOONS)

8 TO 10 (2 POUNDS) BONELESS,
SKINLESS CHICKEN THIGHS

1 CUP KETCHUP

¹/₄ CUP CIDER VINEGAR

¹/₄ CUP PACKED LIGHT
BROWN SUGAR

2 TABLESPOONS CANOLA OIL

1 TABLESPOON
WORCESTERSHIRE SAUCE

1 TEASPOON CHILI POWDER

¹/₂ TEASPOON CHIPOTLE
CHILE POWDER

¹/₂ TEASPOON SALT

12 BUNS

Sprinkle the onion and garlic over the bottom of a 4¹/₂-quart slow cooker; top with the chicken thighs. Stir the ketchup, cider vinegar, brown sugar, canola oil, Worcestershire sauce, chili powder, chipotle chile powder, and salt together in a medium bowl until well blended; pour over the thighs. Cover and cook on low for 8 to 9 hours, until the chicken is fork-tender and easily pulls apart.

Remove the chicken from the slow cooker. In batches, pull it apart into chunks in a shallow dish; return to the slow cooker and stir to combine. Serve spooned into buns, about a scant ¹/₂ cup per bun.

MAKE AHEAD Start this early in the day for an evening potluck or make it completely ahead and refrigerate, covered. Reheat in a large saucepan over medium-low heat, stirring gently, and return to the slow cooker on low heat to keep warm for buffet service.

SERVE WITH Potato chips and pickles, coleslaw, and fresh fruit—the perfect menu for a Super Bowl crowd or a backyard picnic. For dessert, offer brownies and giant oatmeal or snickerdoodle cookies.

While the cooking container isn't the specialty item in this recipe, the rice is. Arborio rice, consisting of short, plump grains full of starch, yields the creamy texture particular to risotto. Adding cooked chicken is an inventive way to use up leftovers and to transform what is traditionally a first-course dish into a main-course offering. The asparagus is an added bonus. Make sure to use real Parmigiano-Reggiano.

Chicken and Asparagus Risotto

✴

2 TABLESPOONS SALTED BUTTER

1 SMALL ONION, CHOPPED (ABOUT 1/2 CUP)

1 CUP ARBORIO RICE

1/2 CUP WHITE WINE

3 1/2 CUPS HOT REDUCED-SODIUM CHICKEN BROTH

1 1/2 CUPS COOKED, CUBED CHICKEN

1 1/2 CUPS COOKED ASPARAGUS CUT IN 1 1/2-INCH PIECES

2 OUNCES PARMIGIANO-REGGIANO, GRATED (ABOUT 1/2 CUP)

1 1/2 TEASPOONS WHITE TRUFFLE OIL, OPTIONAL

Melt the butter in a large, heavy saucepan over medium heat. Add the onion and sauté until tender, about 5 minutes. Add the rice and sauté, stirring often, until the inner kernel appears chalky white, 2 to 3 minutes.

Add the white wine and reduce the heat to medium-low. Stir until the wine is almost absorbed; add 3/4 cup of the chicken broth. Stir until the broth is almost absorbed; repeat three times. Add the final 1/2 cup broth; stir until the liquid is mostly absorbed, but the mixture is still slightly soupy.

Stir in the chicken, asparagus, and Parmesan; cook, gently stirring, until the chicken and asparagus are heated through and the rice is still slightly firm to the bite, 25 to 30 minutes total cooking time. Divide among 4 plates or shallow bowls; drizzle with the truffle oil, if desired, and serve immediately.

MAKE AHEAD Complete the risotto through the second addition of broth and refrigerate, covered, up to several hours in advance of when you are ready to complete the cooking.

SERVE WITH A simple salad dressed very lightly with a lemon and white wine vinegar vinaigrette and some crusty bread.

*B*ack in the 1970s, Americans had a serious love affair with fondue, adopting the Swiss concept as their own. No bridal registry was complete without the ubiquitous fondue pot. Then, like so many cooking fads, fondue disappeared from the culinary scene until it was rediscovered in the 1990s, proving its worth once more as a fun—and easy—way to entertain.

The sauces that follow are quick and simple, but feel free to substitute or supplement with purchased condiments as well. A fruit chutney or a green salsa straight from the grocery shelf are just two possibilities. Use these sauce recipes with the classic oil-cooked beef fondue, too.

Chicken Fondue

MAKES 4 SERVINGS

✳

FOUR 5- TO 6-OUNCE
BONELESS, SKINLESS CHICKEN
BREAST HALVES, CUT IN
3 × 1/2-INCH STRIPS

WOODEN SKEWERS

4 CUPS REDUCED-SODIUM
CHICKEN BROTH

1/4 CUP CHOPPED FRESH CHIVES

1 TABLESPOON CHOPPED
FRESH PARSLEY

ANY OF THE SAUCES
THAT FOLLOW

Thread the chicken strips on the tips of the skewers; arrange on a platter. Heat the chicken broth in a fondue pot until simmering. Stir in the chives and parsley. Cook the skewered chicken in the broth until the chicken is no longer pink in the center when cut with a knife, 5 to 8 minutes. Serve with the sauces of choice.

MAKE AHEAD Make the sauces; cover and refrigerate. Thread the skewers; cover and refrigerate. When ready to serve, heat the broth as indicated and proceed as directed.

SERVE WITH A Caesar salad and crusty French bread.

Lemon Aioli Sauce

1 MEDIUM GARLIC CLOVE, MINCED (ABOUT 1/2 TEASPOON)

1/8 TEASPOON SALT

1/4 CUP MAYONNAISE

1/2 TEASPOON FINELY GRATED LEMON ZEST

1 TEASPOON HEAVY CREAM

Mash the minced garlic and salt together with a fork to make a paste; stir into the mayonnaise in a small bowl. Stir in the lemon zest. Just before serving, thin with the cream.

Lime Chipotle Sauce

1/4 CUP MAYONNAISE

3/4 TEASPOON FINELY MINCED CHIPOTLE CHILE IN ADOBO SAUCE

1 TEASPOON FINELY CHOPPED CILANTRO

3/4 TEASPOON FINELY GRATED LIME ZEST

1 TEASPOON HEAVY CREAM

Stir together the mayonnaise, chipotle chile, cilantro, and lime zest in a small bowl. Just before serving, thin with the cream.

Green Peppercorn and Mustard Sauce

2 TEASPOONS BRINED GREEN PEPPERCORNS, RINSED

1/4 CUP MAYONNAISE

1 TEASPOON DIJON MUSTARD

1 TEASPOON HEAVY CREAM

Mash the green peppercorns with a fork to crush; stir into the mayonnaise in a small bowl. Stir in the mustard. Just before serving, thin with the cream.

Curried Orange Sauce

1/4 CUP PLAIN YOGURT

2 TABLESPOONS ORANGE MARMALADE

1 TEASPOON CURRY POWDER

1/4 TEASPOON GROUND GINGER

PINCH CAYENNE

Stir together the yogurt, orange marmalade, curry powder, ginger, and cayenne in a small bowl.

While it is certainly possible to make paella in a skillet, the special, shallow paella pan that gives this recipe its name cooks everything to perfection. A bit wider than a skillet, at around 14 inches, the pan lets the liquid in the recipe absorb into the rice at the perfect rate. The two handles make moving the pan directly to the table a breeze.

I put this version of paella together for several friends who can't eat shellfish. Instead, chicken and sausage nestle in their bed of rice, enhanced by artichokes and a hint of rosemary. As an alternative for the green beans sometimes included in Valencian recipes, I've chosen sugar snap peas, providing a crisp sweetness and bright color to the final dish.

Paella

MAKES 6 SERVINGS

❊

2 TABLESPOONS OLIVE OIL

1 MEDIUM ONION, CHOPPED (ABOUT 3/4 CUP)

4 BONELESS, SKINLESS CHICKEN THIGHS, CUT IN THIRDS

3 LINKS (ABOUT 1/2 POUND) MILD ITALIAN SAUSAGE, HALVED LENGTHWISE AND CUT IN 2-INCH PIECES (OR SUBSTITUTE A MILD CHICKEN SAUSAGE)

1 RED BELL PEPPER, FINELY CHOPPED (ABOUT 1 1/2 CUPS)

2 LARGE GARLIC CLOVES, CHOPPED (ABOUT 1 TABLESPOON)

2 LARGE ROMA TOMATOES, CHOPPED (ABOUT 1 CUP)

1 TABLESPOON CHOPPED FRESH ROSEMARY

1 1/2 CUPS BOMBA, ARBORIO, OR MEDIUM-GRAIN RICE

Heat the oven to 400°F.

Heat a paella pan or large skillet over medium-high heat; add the olive oil. When hot, add the onion; cook until beginning to soften, stirring frequently, 2 to 3 minutes. Add the chicken and sausage pieces; cook until lightly browned, about 4 minutes per side, scraping the bottom with a wooden spoon occasionally to prevent scorching.

Add the bell pepper and garlic; stir to combine. Add the tomatoes; reduce the heat to medium-low. Cook for 5 minutes; turn the chicken and continue to cook until no longer pink in the thickest portion when cut with a knife, about 5 minutes. Stir in the rosemary and then the rice.

Meanwhile, bring the chicken broth to a boil in a saucepan. (Use only 3 cups if using medium-grain rice.) Remove 1/2 cup of the broth from the pan; add the saffron and stir to dissolve. Add the remaining broth to the paella pan along with the dissolved saffron. Sprinkle with the salt and pepper; stir to combine. Scatter the artichoke hearts into the broth;

increase the heat to medium-high and bring to a boil. Boil for 5 minutes. Place in the oven and bake for 15 minutes. Scatter the sugar snap peas over the rice and press gently into the mixture. Bake for an additional 5 minutes.

MAKE AHEAD Have all the ingredients prepared and assembled in advance.

SERVE WITH A simple tossed salad dressed with an excellent olive oil plus crusty bread.

3 TO 4 CUPS REDUCED-SODIUM
CHICKEN BROTH

3/4 TEASPOON SAFFRON
THREADS, CRUMBLED

1/4 TEASPOON SALT

1/8 TEASPOON FRESHLY
GROUND PEPPER

ONE 9-OUNCE PACKAGE FROZEN
ARTICHOKE HEARTS, THAWED

1 CUP HALVED
SUGAR SNAP PEAS

Using a pressure cooker speeds up the process of cooking dried beans, eliminating any soaking or precooking. The beans initially cook without any acidic ingredients, which can slow their preparation almost to a standstill. Once they are almost tender, the chicken, tomatoes, red wine, and seasonings go in the pot and everything comes together into a lovely soup/stew in short order.

Chicken and Cannellini Bean Stew

MAKES 6 SERVINGS

❊

2 TABLESPOONS OLIVE OIL

1 LARGE ONION, CHOPPED
(ABOUT 1¹/₂ CUPS)

3 MEDIUM CELERY STALKS,
CHOPPED (ABOUT 1 CUP)

3 LARGE GARLIC CLOVES,
CHOPPED (ABOUT
1¹/₂ TABLESPOONS)

1 CUP DRIED CANNELLINI
(WHITE KIDNEY) BEANS, RINSED

6 BONE-IN, SKINLESS CHICKEN
THIGHS

1¹/₂ CUPS BOTTLED MARINARA
SAUCE

ONE 14¹/₂-OUNCE CAN DICED
TOMATOES, DRAINED

¹/₂ CUP RED WINE

2¹/₂ TEASPOONS CHOPPED
FRESH ROSEMARY

¹/₂ TEASPOON SALT

¹/₄ TEASPOON FRESHLY GROUND
PEPPER

¹/₈ TEASPOON CRUSHED DRIED
RED PEPPER FLAKES

¹/₂ CUP CHOPPED FRESH BASIL

Heat the olive oil in the bottom of a pressure cooker over medium heat. Add the onion and celery; sauté until softened, 4 to 5 minutes. Add the garlic; sauté until fragrant, 30 seconds to 1 minute. Add the cannellini beans and 3 cups water. Fasten the lid of the pressure cooker and heat over medium-high heat until the pressure cooker has built up pressure according to the indicator for the model used; reduce the heat to medium-low and cook for 40 minutes. Remove from the heat and wait until the pressure releases enough to allow the cover to be removed, about 15 minutes.

Add the chicken, marinara sauce, tomatoes, red wine, 2 teaspoons of the rosemary, the salt, pepper, and red pepper flakes; stir to blend. Fasten the lid of the pressure cooker and heat over medium-high heat until pressure builds to the appropriate indicator. Reduce the heat to medium-low and cook for 15 minutes. Remove from the heat and wait until the pressure releases enough to allow the lid to be removed, about 15 minutes. Stir in the chopped basil and remaining ¹/₂ teaspoon rosemary; serve.

MAKE AHEAD Make the whole recipe a day or two ahead and refrigerate, covered. Then reheat.

SERVE WITH Crusty bread and a tossed salad with a balsamic vinaigrette. Green beans tossed with olive oil, thyme leaves, and pine nuts would not be amiss.

izutaki is one of several types of *nabemono*, or one-pot, cooking methods in Japanese cuisine. It consists of chicken and vegetables cooked in seasoned water tableside and eaten with a dipping sauce. The traditional pot is a *donabe*, made of clay that can withstand a direct flame, but fondue pots or electric skillets work as well.

Mizutaki

MAKES 4 SERVINGS

❋

ONE 8 × 3-INCH PIECE
KOMBU (SEAWEED)

FOUR 6-OUNCE BONELESS,
SKINLESS CHICKEN BREAST
HALVES, CUT IN 1/2-INCH STRIPS

4 BOK CHOY STALKS,
CUT IN 1 1/2-INCH PIECES
(ABOUT 3 CUPS)

4 OUNCES FRESH SHIITAKE
MUSHROOMS, STEMS REMOVED
AND CAPS SLICED
(ABOUT 2 CUPS)

12 GREEN ONIONS, WHITE AND
TENDER GREEN PORTIONS, CUT
IN 1-INCH LENGTHS

2 LARGE CARROTS, PEELED AND
CUT ON THE DIAGONAL IN
1/4-INCH SLICES
(ABOUT 1 1/2 CUPS)

4 OUNCES SNOW PEAS, CUT IN
THIRDS ON THE DIAGONAL
(ABOUT 1 CUP)

1 CUP PONZU SOY SAUCE
(OR 3/4 CUP SOY SAUCE AND
1/4 CUP LEMON JUICE)

SHREDDED DAIKON RADISH

PICKLED GINGER

2 CUPS COOKED RICE

Tableside, pour 5 cups water into a fondue pot (or 8 cups water into an electric frying pan); add the kombu. Heat to a simmer; simmer for 5 minutes. Remove the kombu and discard.

Arrange the chicken on one plate and the vegetables on a separate platter. Have the diners cook the chicken and vegetables in the simmering water in batches, until the chicken is no longer pink when cut with a knife and the vegetables are crisp-tender, 5 to 8 minutes. Divide the ponzu among 4 small bowls as a dipping sauce, and serve the radish and pickled ginger as condiments.

Finish by ladling the broth over the cooked rice in bowls.

MAKE AHEAD Have all the chicken and vegetables sliced and arranged, then refrigerate, covered. Precook the rice. When ready, heat the water and cook as directed.

SERVE WITH This needs no accompaniment, but cut-up melon would be a refreshing and authentic dessert.

This recipe is a tandoor dish from northern India. *Tikka* translates as "drops" or "round"—a shape that manifests itself as bite-sized kebabs. American kitchens aren't blessed with intense, clay tandoor ovens, but by using the broiler pan as our cooking container of choice, it's possible to approximate a tandoor's quick cooking with little effort.

As an interesting culinary aside, add a tomato-based sauce to Chicken Tikka and it becomes Chicken Tikka Masala, renowned throughout the United Kingdom and considered to be more British than Indian.

Chicken Tikka

MAKES 4 SERVINGS

✳

1/3 CUP PLAIN YOGURT

2 TABLESPOONS LEMON JUICE

1 TABLESPOON CANOLA OIL

2 LARGE GARLIC CLOVES,
MINCED (ABOUT 1 TABLESPOON)

1 TABLESPOON MINCED GINGER

1 TEASPOON GROUND
CORIANDER

3/4 TEASPOON GROUND CUMIN

3/4 TEASPOON GARAM MASALA

1/2 TEASPOON TURMERIC

1/2 TEASPOON SALT

1/8 TEASPOON CAYENNE

FOUR 6-OUNCE BONELESS,
SKINLESS CHICKEN BREAST
HALVES, CUT IN
1 1/2-INCH CUBES

8 WOODEN SKEWERS

Combine the yogurt, lemon juice, canola oil, garlic, ginger, coriander, cumin, garam masala, turmeric, salt, and cayenne in a large, self-sealing plastic bag. Squeeze to blend thoroughly. Add the chicken and squeeze and turn to coat. Marinate in the refrigerator a minimum of 1 hour but up to 12 hours, turning occasionally.

Soak the skewers in water for 30 minutes. Heat the broiler. Thread the marinated chicken on the skewers, leaving a bit of space between the chicken cubes. Arrange on a lightly greased broiler pan. Broil 6 inches from the heat for 8 minutes, turning every 2 minutes, until the chicken is no longer pink in the center when cut with a knife.

MAKE AHEAD Marinate the chicken and thread on the skewers. Refrigerate, covered, until ready to broil.

SERVE WITH Because this dish is often served with cabbage in restaurants, add coleslaw seasoned with cumin and mustard seeds plus basmati rice and naan.

From the time our GIs returned from World War II, pizza has been part of the American dining experience. Now different areas of the United States claim different styles as their own, such as Chicago deep-dish or the California designer-style version. This pizza bianco—meaning without any tomato sauce—is definitely more upscale than your average pepperoni, but still hearty enough to be completely satisfying.

MAKES TWO 14-INCH PIZZAS

✳

CORNMEAL

3 CUPS UNBLEACHED ALL-PURPOSE FLOUR

ONE $1/4$-OUNCE PACKAGE QUICK-RISING YEAST

1 TABLESPOON SUGAR

1 TEASPOON SALT

1 TABLESPOON EXTRA VIRGIN OLIVE OIL

ONE 7-OUNCE CONTAINER PREPARED PESTO

$1/4$ CUP CRÈME FRAÎCHE

1 RED BELL PEPPER, DICED (ABOUT $1^1/2$ CUPS)

$1/2$ CUP CHOPPED GREEN ONIONS

2 CUPS COOKED, DICED CHICKEN

$1/2$ CUP HALVED PITTED KALAMATA OLIVES

$1/2$ CUP PINE NUTS

12 OUNCES MOZZARELLA, SHREDDED (ABOUT 3 CUPS)

$1/4$ CUP COARSELY CHOPPED FRESH BASIL

Chicken and Pesto Pizza

Place the oven racks at the midpoint and lower third of the oven. Heat the oven to 450°F. Lightly grease two pizza pans or cookie sheets; sprinkle them lightly with cornmeal.

Stir together $2^1/2$ cups of the flour, the yeast, sugar, and 3/4 teaspoon of the salt in a medium bowl. Add the olive oil to 1 cup moderately warm water (115°F); stir into the flour mixture to form a soft dough. Sprinkle the counter with a small amount of the remaining flour. Turn out the dough onto the floured counter; knead, adding small amounts of flour as necessary to prevent sticking, until the dough is resilient and barely sticky. Cover and let rise for 15 minutes.

Meanwhile, stir together the pesto, crème fraîche, and remaining $1/4$ teaspoon salt in a small bowl; set aside. Toss together the bell pepper and green onions in a medium bowl; set aside. When the dough has risen, cut it in half and gently shape into two disks, working the dough as little as possible. Sprinkle the counter with any remaining flour or a small amount of additional flour as necessary. Roll each disk into a circle slightly larger than the pizza pan (the dough will shrink when lifted). Place on the prepared pans. Spread each with half of the pesto mixture; sprinkle each with half of the bell pepper mixture. Bake for 4 minutes, staggering the pizzas' location on the oven racks so one pizza is not directly above the other. Rotate one pizza from the middle rack to the lower third and the other from the lower third to the middle. Bake for an additional 4 minutes. Remove from the oven. Top with the chicken, olives, and pine nuts; sprinkle each pizza with half the cheese. Return to the oven and bake for 4 to 6 minutes, until the crust is a rich deep brown. (Remove the bottom pizza first; let the top pizza cook for an additional minute or two.) Sprinkle with the fresh basil; cut into wedges and serve.

MAKE AHEAD Prepare the dough earlier in the day and refrigerate, covered, in a lightly greased bowl. Have all the other ingredients chopped and organized for quick assembly. When ready to assemble the pizzas, punch down the dough and proceed as directed.

SERVE WITH Pizza seems like a stand-alone item, but a nice Caesar salad or tomato-topped tossed salad would not be amiss.

*C*lassic cassoulet is made with a *confit* of duck. To arrive at confit, which means preserved, the duck is first brined and then poached in duck fat. While truly delicious, this is a process most home cooks find a bit too laborious.

I've adapted the concept using chicken. I begin with a kosher chicken, which is already brined. Using the slow cooker and pieces of chicken fat—sold in the same markets as kosher chickens—I've made the confit process quite easy.

I've also streamlined the cassoulet. Instead of dried beans that need soaking and precooking, I use canned beans. The carrot, onion, and garlic take a small, but necessary, detour to a skillet for a quick sauté to soften. The sausage and chicken are browned to bring out their rich flavor, and everything returns to its original pot, the slow cooker, where the recipe finishes countertop.

MAKES 4 SERVINGS

❋

CONFIT OF CHICKEN

2 BONE-IN, SKIN-ON THIGH AND DRUMSTICK PORTIONS AND 2 WINGS FROM A KOSHER CHICKEN (RESERVE THE BREAST FOR ANOTHER USE)

8 OUNCES UNRENDERED CHICKEN FAT

1/2 TEASPOON DRIED THYME

1/4 TEASPOON COARSE, FRESHLY GROUND PEPPER

1/2 CUP REDUCED-SODIUM CHICKEN BROTH

Cassoulet

For the confit of chicken, arrange the chicken pieces in the bottom of a 4¹/2-quart slow cooker; layer with the chicken fat. Sprinkle with the thyme and pepper; pour the chicken broth over all. Cook on the low setting for 5 hours; remove the chicken pieces, which are now confit. Strain the fat and broth into a bowl; separate the fat from the broth.

For the cassoulet, heat the confit fat in a medium skillet over medium-low heat. Add the onion and carrot; sauté until softened, 6 to 8 minutes. Stir in the garlic; sauté for 1 minute. Remove from the heat; stir in the confit broth, tomato paste, thyme, salt, and pepper. Add the beans and gently mix. Spoon into the slow cooker. Add the sausage pieces to the same skillet and increase the heat to medium-high. Brown lightly on all sides; 6 to 8 minutes total. Remove to the slow cooker. Add the confit of chicken to the skillet and brown lightly, 2 to 3 minutes per side. Remove to the slow cooker. Cover and cook on the high setting for 1 hour.

MAKE AHEAD Make the confit portion of the recipe the day before. Refrigerate the confit of chicken, covered. Refrigerate the fat and broth together in the bowl; spoon off the fat when congealed. Complete the recipe the following day.

SERVE WITH Crusty bread and a tossed salad topped with toasted walnuts.

CASSOULET

2 TABLESPOONS CONFIT FAT

1 MEDIUM ONION, CHOPPED (ABOUT 3/4 CUP)

1 LARGE CARROT, PEELED AND CHOPPED (ABOUT 3/4 CUP)

4 LARGE GARLIC CLOVES, CHOPPED (ABOUT 2 TABLESPOONS)

6 TABLESPOONS CONFIT BROTH

2 TABLESPOONS TOMATO PASTE

1/2 TEASPOON DRIED THYME

1/2 TEASPOON SALT

1/4 TEASPOON FRESHLY GROUND PEPPER

TWO 15.8-OUNCE CANS GREAT NORTHERN BEANS, DRAINED AND RINSED

1/2 POUND CURED SAUSAGE, SUCH AS POLISH KIELBASA, CUT IN 2-INCH PIECES

*S*moked chicken stands in for the more usual ham and contrasts well with the sweet taste of fresh spring peas. I've fudged a bit by sautéing the onions and baby portobello mushrooms in a skillet before adding them to the quiche, but they taste so much better that I think this step is important in what is still, essentially, a one-dish meal.

I make my crust in the classic French fashion with butter, but feel free to use lard or solid vegetable shortening instead. Each produces a slightly different texture and taste to the finished product, with butter making the crispest crust and lard the flakiest.

Smoked Chicken and Spring Pea Quiche

MAKES 6 FIRST-COURSE OR LUNCHEON SERVINGS, OR 4 MAIN-COURSE SERVINGS

❋

CRUST

1¼ CUPS ALL-PURPOSE FLOUR

¼ TEASPOON SALT

8 TABLESPOONS (1 STICK) CHILLED UNSALTED BUTTER, CUT IN BITS

For the crust, combine the flour and salt in a bowl. Cut in the butter with your fingertips or a pastry cutter, until the mixture resembles a combination of coarse sand and small pebbles. Toss with 2 to 3 tablespoons ice water, using just enough water to bring the mixture together in a ball. Wrap in plastic wrap, flatten into a disk, and refrigerate for 1 hour.

Heat the oven to 425°F. Roll out the dough on a lightly floured surface to a scant ¼-inch thickness. Place the dough in a 9-inch tart pan with a removable bottom. Press the dough around the edges downward to firm the sides. Trim the excess dough and reserve the scraps. Line the dough with aluminum foil; weight the bottom with dried beans, rice, or pie weights. Bake for 13 to 15 minutes, until the dough is set. Remove the foil and weights; bake for an additional 5 to 6 minutes, until lightly browned. If the dough has cracked during baking, let the crust cool slightly, then patch it by pressing some of the reserved scraps of dough gently into the cracks.

For the filling, while the crust is baking, melt the butter in a medium skillet over medium heat. Add the green onions;

sauté for 1 minute. Add the mushrooms; sauté until softened, 4 to 5 minutes. Remove from the heat; stir in the peas. Set aside.

Reduce the oven temperature to 375°F. Place the tart pan in an aluminum foil–lined, shallow baking pan. Scatter the chicken over the bottom of the crust; sprinkle evenly with the Gruyère. Top with the mushroom-and-pea mixture. Whisk the eggs together in a medium bowl to blend; whisk in the crème fraîche, heavy cream, salt, pepper, and nutmeg. Pour slowly into the tart pan. Bake for 30 to 35 minutes, until browned, slightly puffed, and a knife inserted in the center comes out clean.

MAKE AHEAD The nice thing about quiche is that it is also good served at room temperature. Make the quiche up to several hours in advance; refrigerate. Reheat in a 350°F oven until just warmed through, 15 to 25 minutes, or let come to room temperature before serving.

SERVE WITH Crusty bread plus spring greens tossed with a mustard vinaigrette.

FILLING

2 TABLESPOONS SALTED OR UNSALTED BUTTER

1/3 CUP CHOPPED GREEN ONIONS

1 CUP SLICED BABY PORTOBELLO (CREMINI) MUSHROOMS

3/4 CUP SHELLED FRESH PEAS (OR FROZEN AND THAWED)

1 CUP DICED SMOKED CHICKEN

1 CUP SHREDDED GRUYÈRE (ABOUT 4 OUNCES)

3 LARGE EGGS

1/2 CUP CRÈME FRAÎCHE

1/4 CUP HEAVY CREAM

3/4 TEASPOON SALT

1/4 TEASPOON FRESHLY GROUND PEPPER

PINCH GROUND NUTMEG

CubanFoodMarket.com
www.cubanfoodmarket.com
Goya brand Mojo Criollo marinade

EthnicGrocer.com
www.ethnicgrocer.com
Lee Kum Kee brand of:
  Black bean sauce
  Chili garlic sauce
  Hoisin sauce
  Oyster sauce
  Sesame oil
Plus many other Asian ingredients, including:
  Dried lemongrass
  Fish sauce
  Green curry paste
  Kombu (Konbu)
  Panko bread crumbs
  Pickled ginger

Pacific Rim Gourmet
www.pacificrimgourmet.com
Five-spice powder
Green curry paste
Kombu
Ponzu soy sauce
Yellow curry paste

Penzeys Spices
1–800–741–7787
www.penzeys.com
Aleppo pepper
Annatto seeds
Garam masala
Ground sumac
Herbes de Provence
Sweet Hungarian paprika

Temple of Thai
www.templeofthai.com
Fish sauce
Green curry paste
Yellow curry paste

La Tienda
1–888–472–1022
www.tienda.com
Bomba rice
Serrano ham
Plus cooking equipment, including:
  Cazuelas
  Paella pans

BIBLIOGRAPHY

Bayless, Rick, with Deann Groen Bayless. *Authentic Mexican*. New York: William Morrow & Company, Inc., 1987.

Becker, Marion Rombauer, et al. *The All New All Purpose Joy of Cooking*, revised edition. New York: Scribner, 1997.

Burdick, Jacques. *Savory Stews*. New York: Fawcett Columbine, 1995.

Caggiano, Biba. *From Biba's Italian Kitchen*. New York: Hearst Corporation, 1995.

Cecconi, Antonio. *Betty Crocker's Italian Cooking*. Foster City, CA: IDG Books Worldwide, 2000.

———. *Betty Crocker's New Italian Cooking*. New York: Macmillan, 1994.

Chin, Leeann. *Betty Crocker's Chinese Cookbook*. New York: Random House, Inc., 1981.

Gulden, Diana. *Betty Crocker's New International Cookbook*, revised edition. New York: Prentice-Hall General, 1989.

Harris, Jessica B. *The Africa Cookbook: Tastes of a Continent*. New York: Simon & Schuster, 1998.

Helou, Anissa. *Street Café Morocco*. London: Conran Octopus Limited, 1998.

Herbst, Sharon Tyler *The New Food Lover's Companion*, second edition. Hauppauge, N.Y.: Barron's Educational Series, Inc., 1995.

Iyer, Raghavan. *Betty Crocker's Indian Home Cooking*. New York: Hungry Minds, Inc., 2001.

———. *The Turmeric Trail: Recipes and Memories from an Indian Childhood*. New York: St. Martin's Press, 2002.

Kasper, Lynne. *The Italian Country Table: Home Cooking from Italy's Farmhouse Kitchens*. New York: Scribner, 1999.

Kremezi, Aglaia. *The Foods of the Greek Islands: Cooking and Culture at the Crossroads of the Mediterranean*. Boston: Houghton Mifflin, 2000.

Laurendon, Laurence et Giles. *Recettes & autres histories de poules*. Paris: Marabout (Hachette Livre), 2001.

Leonard, Jonathan Norton. *Time-Life Latin American Cooking (Foods of the World Series)*. New York: Time-Life Books, 1979.

Levy, Faye. *Faye Levy's International Chicken Book*. New York: Warner Books, Inc., 1992.

National Council of Negro Women, Inc. *The Black Family Reunion Cookbook: Recipes & Food Memories*. Memphis: The Wimmer Companies, 1991.

Ortiz, Elizabeth Lambert. *The Complete Book of Caribbean Cooking*. New York: Ballantine Books, 1973.

————. *The Food of Spain and Portugal: The Complete Iberian Cuisine*. New York: Atheneum, 1989.

Parragon Publishing. *Practical Cooking: Chicken*. Bath, England: Parragon Publishing, 2001.

Raichlen, Steven. *Steven Raichlen's Healthy Latin Cooking: 200 Sizzling Recipes from Mexico, Cuba, Caribbean, Brazil, and Beyond*. Emmaus, Pa.: Rodale Books, 2000.

Sunset Books. *The Best of Sunset: Over 500 All-Time Favorite Recipes from the Magazine of Western Living*. Menlo Park, Calif.: Lane, 1987.

Wolfert, Paula. *The Cooking of the Eastern Mediterranean: 215 Healthy, Vibrant, and Inspired Recipes*. New York: HarperCollins, 1994.

————. *Couscous and Other Good Food from Morocco*. New York: Harper & Row, 1973.

Wright, Clifford A. *Real Stew: 300 Recipes for Authentic Home-Cooked Cassoulet, Gumbo, Chili, Curry, Minestrone, Bouillabaisse, Stroganoff, Goulash, Chowder, and Much More*. Boston: Harvard Common Press, 2002.